HOW TO TELL YOUR FRIENDS
FROM THE APES

*

Will Cuppy

———

HOW
TO TELL YOUR FRIENDS
FROM THE APES

With an Introduction by
P. G. Wodehouse

Illustrated by Jacks

LIVERIGHT New York · London

ISBN 0-87140-134-7

Liveright Publishing Corporation, 500 Fifth Avenue,
New York, N.Y. 10110

9 0

ACKNOWLEDGMENTS

For permission to reprint certain portions of his text the author thanks THE NEW YORKER *and* COLLEGE HUMOR. *He has added sundry jests which were considered too funny for magazine publication.*

INTRODUCTION
BY P. G. WODEHOUSE

*

WILL Cuppy, who wrote all of this book except this introduction, is a young—or what greybeards like myself consider young—American writer with, at the moment of going to press, three claims to fame. He can tell his friends from the Apes (which not many of us can do). He is the author of the best thing said about Pekingese, viz. 'I don't see why they should look so conceited. They're no better than we are.' And he has been for so many years America's leading reviewer of detective stories that, though he has never actually murdered a Baronet in his library, he knows fifty-seven ways of doing it and throwing suspicion on the butler. Mystery writers may befog thousands, but they cannot befog Will Cuppy. He is the man who always guesses right at the end of Chapter Two.

There is always something a little tricky in composing an introduction to a book like this. Critics are touchy, and if I say that it is one of the funniest I have ever read they may purse their lips and suggest that statements of that kind are better left to them. I will confine my remarks, therefore, to the volume's usefulness, a quality which, I imagine, nobody will seriously deny.

How often we have been at a dinner where the partner on our right has suddenly said to us, 'And now, Mr. Robinson, (or Mr. Abbott), I want you to tell me all about penguins,' and had us gasping for air and crumbling bread. Mr. Cuppy has removed all danger of further embarrassment of that kind. A glance at our copy of *How To Tell Your Friends From The Apes*, which we have concealed in our napkin, and we are replying confidently:

Penguins are dignified. To catch a penguin off its dignity might take years and would hardly be worth the trouble. The average penguin has the mind of an eight-year old child, but he gets his name in the papers. Only the expert can tell a live penguin from a stuffed one. It is probable that most penguins are stuffed.

Scarcely are the words out of our mouth when the partner on our left, archly tapping our wrist with her fan, says: 'And tigers, Mr. Fosberry?' To which, like a flash:

(6)

Tigers live in Asia in nullahs and sholahs. They seldom climb trees, but don't count on that. Young normal tigers do not eat people. If eaten by a tiger, you may rest assured that it is abnormal. Once in a while a normal tiger will eat somebody, but he doesn't mean anything by it.

I quote this last passage with pleasure, for I like its kindly broadmindedness. Elsewhere in the book Mr. Cuppy is inclined at times to write a little caustically. Now and then his tone is that of a disillusioned man who has met too many rhinoceri and hippopotami—or perhaps not just the right sort of rhinoceri and hippopotami. It is so fatally easy to judge a species from the individual, and when Mr. Cuppy says of the rhinoceros that its expression lacks all charm and its profile is utterly hopeless, we sense the bitterness of the man who has had unfortunate dealings with some particular rhinoceros and has allowed himself to become biased.

But even where we disagree with Mr. Cuppy we cannot but admire his frankness and fearlessness. He says things boldly, regardless of how he may be conflicting with vested interests, things which more timid souls have been content merely to think.

'What this country needs,' he says, nailing his colours to the mast, 'is a good medium-priced giraffe.'

If I have thought that once, I have thought it a hundred times, but always a fear of giving offence to the powerful Giraffe Ring has kept me from speaking out. And I doubt whether even Mr. Cuppy's trumpet-blast will have much effect. As he himself points out:

When standing beside a mimosa the giraffe is indistinguishable from the tree, except that he has four legs and a head and a tail. Some hunters will stalk a mimosa tree for days without getting results.

This all adds to the overhead, and will probably be advanced by the Ring as an excuse for keeping the price up. (Fifteen thousand dollars apiece is what they are asking, in case you are interested. Personally, I simply won't pay it.)

Coming back to the subject of Introductions, another difficulty about writing them is that you never know how much of the book you can quote. If you quote it all, it is obviously mere waste of money for the publishers to print anything except the Introduction: and yet I find it very hard not to quote all of *How To Tell Your Friends From The Apes.* Perhaps the best plan will be for me to now conclude, hoping that this finds you in the pink, as it leaves me.

Hippopotamuses live in herds, even though this involves being with other hippopotamuses. The crow . . .

No. I must be firm. I will now conclude.

P. G. WODEHOUSE

PREFACE

*

I HAVE been asked several times just what I mean by writing another book. I'm not sure that I mean anything in particular. People have been known to write dozens of books. This is only my second. So much for that.

And then the title. Why did I call the book "How To Tell Your Friends From the Apes" when I could so easily have called it "Random Gleanings From the Natural History of the Early Assyrians"? Well, that title had already been used. So had "Outlines of Comparative Physiology."

I still mourn for "Outlines of Comparative Physiology." There's a title that has everything: grace, sparkling wit, scientific significance and as much sex appeal as you can bring to it. Talk about romance!

Other titles were dropped for various reasons. You may think that people will let you call your own book "Notes on the Larger Fauna of the Strait of Magellan, Western Patagonia and Tierra del Fuego." Well, they won't! And I can see now that "Is the Horse Doomed?" was no name for a zoölogical work aiming to deal with practically all of our dumb brothers. Besides, we all know that the Horse is doomed. Why keep rubbing it in?

Things went on like that most of the summer, until one day—that terrifically hot day—something seemed to snap, and I knew that I had been writing "How Dante Became the World's Most Famous Book-end." Since then I have agreed to a few slight changes in the wording.

Certain persons have asked me whether the title as it now appears is a steal from "How To Tell the Birds From the Flowers," by Robert Williams Wood, a sterling little volume in verse and pictures published in 1917 and still going strong. To this somewhat tactless inquiry I have decided to answer yes. Why argue the point?

The truth is that I have long regarded Mr. Wood's book as a step in the right direction. We need more and yet more of these how-to-tell books, for isn't it high time that we learned to tell a few things apart in this topsy-turvy old world? Let's have more light on the subject, then. Let's start right now and see who can tell the most things apart. In that way we may get somewhere.

Now about my central problem. Ninety per cent of the adult humans examined by me stated that they had never found any difficulty in telling their friends from the Apes. I wonder if some of these good people aren't kidding themselves? The other ten per cent refused either to face the facts or to be pinned down about buying the book. In several instances I got the distinct impression that I was dealing with Gibbons.

I grant you there are plenty of old-fashioned and pretty ineffective ways to tell one's friends from the Apes. What could be simpler, for instance, when you are at the Zoo? The Apes are in cages.

Yes, but when you are *not* at the Zoo, what then?

As for my style, as represented in my brief and all-of-a-piece biographies, an acquaintance wishes to know if I intend to go on writing in chunks for the rest of my life? That is a matter I have not yet decided. I may, and I may not. How on earth does one know whether or not one is going to go on writing in chunks?

Nor must I omit the usual acknowledgments. During my labors I found time for my first intensive study of Aristotle, whose "History of Animals" provided me with a footnote or two. The more one peruses this author, and ponders upon him, the more one realizes the wide range, the almost universal scope of his misinformation. I cannot help thinking that is why his pupil, Alexander the Great, was so simple in some respects. You know what the Intelligence Tests showed during the War; and isn't that the answer to everything, when you come right down to it? I fancy that conditions in Ancient Greece weren't a whole lot different.

Fortunately, there are others. Elsewhere in this volume I have confessed my not inconsiderable indebtedness to Isabel Paterson. From my frequent debates with her about the animals, I gathered whatever in these little sketches may prove of lasting worth. A reviewer of "How To Be a Hermit" said that he had long regarded the undersigned as a figment of Isabel Paterson's imagination. I could wish that this legend might persist, for I know of nobody at all of whose imagination I should feel prouder and more signally honored to be a figment.

In closing I would say that if I have succeeded, however imperfectly, in my efforts to amuse, if I have served to while away an idle hour, if I have caught within these pages aught of profit or of pleasure—in short, if I have written the best book of the season, I shall be very much surprised.

CONTENTS

*

MEMOIRS OF THE JUKES FAMILY

or

WHERE WE COME IN

*

THE JAVA MAN

THE PEKING MAN

THE PILTDOWN MAN

THE HEIDELBERG MAN

THE NEANDERTHAL MAN

THE CRO-MAGNON MAN

THE MODERN MAN

THE JAVA MAN

T HE Java Man lived in Java 500,000 or 1,000,-
000 or 2,000,000 years ago [1] and was lower than
we are. He was Lower Pleistocene and Lower Quar-
ternary and knock-kneed. He was called *Pithecanthropus* ("Ape-Man") *erectus* because he walked
with a slight stoop. The Java Man consisted of a calvarium, three teeth and a femur belonging to himself
or two other Ape-Men. Professor Dubois made him

a face which proves that he was dolichocephalic or long-headed instead of brachycephalic or square-headed and that he was 5 feet 6½ inches high and that Barnum was right. The Java Man was more Manlike than Apelike and more Apelike than Manlike. He had immense supraorbital ridges of solid bone and was conscious in spots. Does that remind you of any one? [2] His Broca's area was low. He could say that the evenings were drawing in and times were hard and his feet hurt. The spiritual life of the Java Man was low because he was only a beginner. He was just a child at heart and was perfectly satisfied with his polygamy, polygyny, polyandry, endogamy, exogamy, totemism and nymphomania. How he ever became extinct is beyond me. The Java Man has been called the Missing Link by those who should know.

[1] Or 250,000 or 750,000.
[2] Sir Arthur Keith says that *Pithecanthropus erectus* was human in everything but the brain. Well, what did he expect?

THE Peking Man shows that people were living in Asia long long ago as most of us knew already. He was discovered near Peking or Peiping and was named *Sinanthropus pekinensis* to keep certain persons from calling him Peiping Tom. *Sin* means China although the Chinese are no worse than other foreigners. The glabella was prominent so he was probably a young male.[1] The brain shows that the calvarium or brain-case was good. The skull was in perfect condition because the Peking Man took better care of his skull than some of us. He had begun to think or whatever the Chinese do. The prefrontal region resembles that found in some parts of the Middle West. The right horizontal ramus shows a tendency to do everything backwards. The Peking Man is lovable because he left no culture. He knew nothing about the Ming Dynasty and the Ch'ing Dynasty and the Sung Dynasty and he wrote no short poems stating that he got drunk and went out in a canoe and fell in. He had no imports and exports but he had fauna and flora.[2] The Peking Man was fond of overpopulation. We do not know whether he was religious or promiscuous or both. He did not have love as we understand it because he had no gin.

[1] Or a young female.
[2] He had the Catalpa, the Soy Bean, the Mongolian Mammoth, the Chinese Ostrich, the Yak and the Carp. He may have had Bats.

THE PILTDOWN MAN

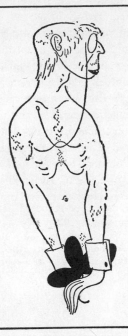

THE Piltdown Man was called the Dawn Man or Barmy Ned because he was found in Great Britain. He was a great help because he left crude flint implements. These were small rough pebbles chipped by the Piltdown Man just as all the small rough pebbles of today were chipped by us. Crude flint implements were used for making still cruder flint implements.[1] The Piltdown Man had little to do. His skull was twice as thick as an ordinary Englishman. It is in small pieces which can be fitted together in various ways after choosing sides. This is called Badminton. He could collect stamps. The Piltdown Man had aspidistras, delphiniums and sinus trouble. Already he was aiming at the stars and missing them. The manubrium indicates self-control but very little to control. The Piltdown Man had no chin and was rather toothy. It seems incredible that he had a private life but those are just the ones who do. The young took after their parents. Anthropologists say that the Piltdown Man was stupider than any person of today. Anthropologists are people who are in museums. They lead sheltered lives. The Early Irish left few skulls. The Early Scotch left no skulls.

[1] Some say the Piltdown Man also used them to scrape furs if he had furs, for clothing if he had clothing. It is not improbable that the better sort of Piltdown Men employed some form of covering, if only a minimum.

THE Heidelberg Man was known as the Heidelberg Jaw. He had more jaw than any other male fossil. Professor Schoetensack had been saying for twenty years that he would find just such a jaw and you can bet that he did. The Heidelberg Man developed his jaw by agglutinative language and umlauts. He did this once too often and became extinct. The Heidelberg Man lived on plain simple food and good fresh air.

(23)

He had toothache, indigestion and dizzy spells. He had brains in all the wrong places. If you asked him a question he would answer some other question. He had a vestigial tail and so have some other people I might mention. The Heidelberg Man was a Nudist and he was fond of companionship. He chose his companions by trial and error. He did not keep track of them all because he had no adding machine. He believed that practice makes perfect.[1] His wit and humor ran to practical jokes such as pushing other Heidelberg Men off the Alps and hitting them in the eye with large rocks or Paleoliths.[2] He was almost always angry and ferocious, causing an increased flow of adrenalin from the suprarenal capsules into the bloodstream. This could not go on forever. There were good ones and bad ones.[3]

[1] In this species the male was the boss.
[2] There has been some doubt whether the Heidelberg Man talked. Of course he talked. You couldn't stop him.
[3] The Heidelberg Man was the first fossil who could be called Man in Latin, so he was called *Homo heidelbergensis*. The Java, Peking and Piltdown Men could only be called Men in English.

THE NEANDERTHAL MAN

THE Neanderthal Man lived in fear of the Woolly Mammoth, the Woolly Rhinoceros, the Woolly Hyena [1] and the Neanderthal Woman, who would drag him to her cave and roll great stones against the door and marry him. The Neanderthal Woman had no charm but she had a club. The Neanderthal Man was so difficult to rouse that one wonders if it was worth it. There were no icemen because it was the Great Ice

Age. Neanderthal Men had very short fibulas. They walked with a shuffling gait like Edgar Wallace characters. They were slow on the uptake. The Neanderthals lived in groups under an Old Man who would drive out all the likely youths as soon as they were likely. Then the more intelligent girls would stroll off in the same direction to pick wild flowers. They would have clubs. The Neanderthal Man had plenty of brains but somehow they did him no good. During the Great Ice Age the glaciers kept advancing and retreating much more than they do now. They kept the Neanderthals on the run. The glaciers were in a wild state and only the fleetest Neanderthals could escape from them.[2] This was the survival of the fleetest. The Neanderthal Man had fires, caves, marrow bones,[3] mosquitoes, love and arthritis. What more can you ask?

[1] The Neanderthal Man was rather woolly himself.
[2] Cf. "Pursued by a Glacier."
[3] Neanderthal Men also ate Snails, Frogs, Lemmings and other varmints. Some say they ate fried Neanderthal.

THE Cro-Magnons were an old man, two young men, a woman and a child. The woman's brain was larger than the average man's. She had been killed with a blunt implement. The Cro-Magnons were very tall and had perfectly enormous fibulas like those in Chicago and Minneapolis, caused by chromosomes, genes, hormones and blastomeres. They were so wonderful that they were called *Homo sapiens* after us. They had Adam's apples. The Cro-Magnons were Upper Pleistocene and respectable. They invented Santa Claus, foreign missions, eggplant, punctuation, tatting and new methods of killing Neanderthals. They made rules preventing each other from doing what they did. We should love the Cro-Magnons because they were so smug.[1] The Cro-Magnons were interested in art because of their unhappy home life which in turn was caused by their art. They would paint a Woolly Rhinoceros or a Paleolithic Bison in a cave when there was no one to stop them. Their favorite painting was called "A Yard of Paleolithic Bison." Their art was Independent and was finally arrested. It was Late Aurignacian because it was found in Early Solutrean deposits. The Cro-Magnons died out because they neglected sex.

[1] Perhaps we of today are inclined to overestimate the intellectual powers of the Cro-Magnons, who lived at least 25,000 years ago. As some of my readers may recall, even so recently as twenty or thirty years ago people knew hardly anything. For earlier data one has but to glance at the Family Album.

THE MODERN MAN

THE Modern Man or Nervous Wreck is the highest of all mammals because anyone can see that he is. There are about 2,000,000,000 Modern Men or too many. The Modern Man's highly developed brain has made him what he is and you know what he is.[1] The development of his brain is caused by his upright or bipedal position, as in the Penguin, the Dinosaur and other extinct reptiles. Modern Man has been called the Talking Animal because he talks more than any three other animals chosen at random. He has also been called the Reasoning Animal but there may be a catch in this. The fissure of Sylvius and the fissure of Rolando enable him to argue in circles. His main pursuits in the order named are murder, robbery, kidnapping, body-snatching, barratry, nepotism, arson and mayhem. This is known as the Good, the True and the Beautiful. Modern Men are viviparous. They mature slowly but make up for it later, generally from July first to June thirtieth inclusive. The females carry nickels and pins in their mouths. They are fond of glittering objects, bits of ribbon and olives.[2] All Modern Men are descended from a Wormlike creature but it shows more on some people. Modern Man will never become extinct if the Democrats can help it.[3]

[1] It is because of his brain that he has risen above the animals. Guess which animals he has risen above.

[2] Each male has from 2 to 790 females with whom he discusses current events. Of these he marries from 3 to 17.

[3] To be perfectly fair, Modern Man was invented on October 25, 4004 B.C., at 9 o'clock in the morning, according to the statement of Dr. John Lightfoot (1602-1675) of Stoke-upon-Trent, Vice-chancellor of the University of Cambridge. Dr. Lightfoot's *Whole Works* comes in thirteen volumes.

HOW TO TELL YOUR FRIENDS
FROM THE APES
or
A MONKEY A DAY

*

THE CHIMPANZEE

THE GORILLA

THE ORANG-UTAN

THE GIBBON

THE BABOON

THE HOWLING MONKEY

THE LEMUR

THE CHIMPANZEE

THE Chimpanzee[1] is found in Equatorial Africa and vaudeville. He is the brightest of the Anthropoid Apes because he is so classified by scientists with incomes over five thousand dollars. If the scientist places a banana in a box the Chimpanzee will go and get it and eat it. The Chimpanzee also likes hominy, lettuce, raspberries, weak tea and black beetles. Chimpanzees are highly excitable and partly web-footed. They are amusing but terribly shallow. They can be very trying. The love life of Chimpanzees is about what you might expect. When a Chimpanzee looks at another Chimp he does not see what we see. They frequently have twins. Male Chimpanzees are called Soko or Bam. Females are called Malapunga. Chimpanzee sweethearts say very little. They can say "Yes" and "No" and "Thank you very much." [2] They can count up to five. They are faithful within reason. In the Chimpanzee the hallux is opposable and the pollex is not. In Man it is just the other way round so it all comes out even. The Chimpanzee smokes, rides a bicycle and wears pants. His chief ambition is to play the Palace. The Chimpanzee has one-third enough brain and that's something. Or is it?

[1] Aristotle did not mention Chimps but they got along somehow.

[2] What they really say is *gak gak, ngak ngak* and *wha wha.* Chimpanzees find these words sufficient for all practical purposes.

THE GORILLA

AFTER a Chimp the Gorilla is a great relief. He is fierce and brutal and is not a mimic. He weighs 450 pounds and is named Bobby. Young Gorillas are friendly but they soon learn. When a banana is placed in a trick box within easy reach the Gorilla will bite the professor's cousin. Guess what that proves. The Gorilla is becoming extinct but there are plenty of professors. In affairs of the heart the male Gorilla is slow but sure. He appears to be stolid and indifferent but that may be part of his system.[1] Believe it or not he is shy. The Gorilla is an introvert. Married females and their children sleep in trees and the male sleeps on the ground. The meaning of this is unknown. The Gorilla could do with more brains. His corpus callosum is not very good but the hippocampus major is O. K. The hallux is fair. Gorillas like sugar-cane, hay, watermelons, ragout of chicken, raw ham, dandelions and lollypops. They are subject to inflammation of the gums. Female Gorillas are likely to bump into passing objects and have trouble with revolving doors. I am in favor of Gorillas. They live in Africa.[2]

[1] The Gorilla is said to have hidden depths, but if they are so hidden what good are they? He has small ears, generally a bad sign.

[2] They have a nasty habit of biting shotguns.

THE ORANG-UTAN

ORANG-UTANS teach us that looks are not every-thing but darned near it.[1] They look awful. Some Orang-utans have huge cheek pads and conspicuous laryngeal sacs. Others have worse. The hallux is un-developed. The female is not so ugly but ugly enough. Both sexes brood a lot. Their prolonged spells of medi-tation appear to have no tangible results. Orangs often sleep on one arm and wake up with a cramp. They snore. Young Orangs who are permitted to develop their individualities turn out horribly. Young Orangs who are kicked and beaten into line also turn out horribly. The psychology of the Orang-utan has been thoroughly described by scientists from their observation of the Sea-urchin. Other facts have been gathered from the natives of Borneo and Sumatra who may have been talking about something else at the time. There is considerable doubt whether the Orang-utan is as dumb as he seems or dumber. He likes stewed apples, toast, cocoa and soap. Orang-utans have solved the problem of work. They do not work. They never worry. And yet they have wrinkles. So what's the use?

[1] About 93 per cent.

THE GIBBON

THOSE thin long-waisted types with no head to speak of are generally Gibbons. Gibbons are our loudest Apes. Their peculiar cry is often described as *hoo hoo hoo hoo* and just as often as *whopp whopp whopp whopp*. Gibbons assemble in crowds and *hoo* or *whopp* until exhausted or shot. The natives of Cochin China, the Malay Archipelago and the Island of Hainan often have *hoo* or *whopp* madness. A noise-less Gibbon would be a godsend. There is an old say-ing that the Gibbon is at his best in the American Museum of Natural History.[1] The female Wau-wau or Silvery Gibbon of Java is rather pretty for a Wau-wau. The Hoolock of Upper Assam cannot swim. Gib-bons are noted for the number and variety of things they cannot do. It is believed that the Gibbon could be taught to swat flies. Gibbons live in the treetops. They swing from branch to branch by their arms with amaz-ing speed. They are not going to fires. They are going nowhere in particular. Experiments with the Gibbon prove many interesting things about the Long-nosed Bandicoot. Gibbon authorities do not know whether the Gibbon is interested in sex. But you know and I know. There are no Apes in this country, thank good-ness.[2]

[1] Cf. "Decline and Fall of the Gibbon."
[2] Embalmed Gibbons are sometimes sold to country bump-kins as embalmed Pigmies. Why our rural population should prefer embalmed Pigmies to embalmed Gibbons offers an in-teresting problem in psychology.

THE BABOON

THE Baboon is entirely uncalled for. Some people like Baboons but something is wrong with such people. Baboons lose their tempers. There are more Baboons than you might think. The Baboon is not an Anthropoid Ape. He has a tail, though not a good one, and so he is a Lower Ape. In fact he is more of a Monkey. The Arabian Baboon as the name implies is found in Abyssinia. Baboons have highly colored ischial callosities. Scientists tell us that all animals who sit down a great deal have ischial callosities. That is a lie. The Mandrill is the worst especially when going South. Baboons bark. It seems as though there would be no female Baboons but there are. The family life of the Baboon is known as hell on earth. The males grow meaner and stingier and the females fade at an early age. The children scream, stamp, roll on the ground and will not eat their Centipedes. Their parents are proud of them.[1] The Sacred Baboon of the Egyptians was identified with Thoth, the god of literary criticism.[2] He spent his time making Thothlike motions at the Sacred Ibis, another form of literary criticism. He is not yet extinct. Never call anyone a Baboon unless you are sure of your facts. Baboons have flat feet.

[1] Young Baboons ride pick-a-back.
[2] He is frequently pictured restoring the Udjat or Eye to Aah, the Moon God. Enormous numbers of Udjats have been found in Ancient Egyptian tombs. "The twin Udjats represent the Eye of the Sun and the Eye of the Moon."—Sir E. A. Wallis Budge.

THE HOWLING MONKEY

THE Howling Monkey is confined to South America but seems to escape. The back of his head is straight up and down. His howl is caused by a large hyoid bone at the top of the trachea. It can be cured by a simple operation on the neck with an axe. The male Howler is always followed by seven or eight female Howlers with young Howlers but this may be a coincidence. Howlers have long prehensile tails with which they hang from the trees, talk Monkey talk and pick up Brazil nuts. There are several species of Howlers. The Fat Howler is as trying as any. The Howling Monkey and the Spider Monkey are neighbors. The infant Howling Monkey occasionally bears a striking resemblance to a Spider Monkey. Ask me sometime why that is.[1] The Capuchin or Organ Grinder Monkey is regarded as very intelligent. He scrambles after pennies, scratches himself and has morals. He can stand on his hind legs but the tail is a dead giveaway.[2] Monkeys have loads of fun. They breed in captivity and know many other tricks. They are fond of Bats, marshmallows, Goldfish and ink. Old World Monkeys cannot hang by their tails. They might as well not be Monkeys.[3]

[1] Spider Monkeys look nothing like Spiders.
[2] The Tee-tee or Squirrel Monkey inhabits Brazil and the Reading Room of the British Museum.
[3] There is a general feeling among Old World Monkeys that they are the best Monkeys, but there is no scientific basis for this. If you are an Old World Monkey you are classed as Catarrhine or narrow-nosed. If not, you are Platyrrhine or broad-nosed. That's about the gist of it.

THE LEMUR

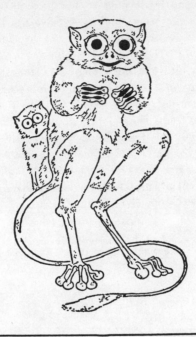

THE Lemur is one worse than the Monkey. He **is**
often mistaken for **a** Squirrel, a Rabbit, an
Agouti or anything but a Lemur. He has been described as a state of mind or ectoplasm. The Lemur
is a Primate because people say so. The Lemur sleeps
all day long and nobody tells him that be is a tramp.
When disturbed he sort of squeaks. Most Lemurs live

(45)

in Madagascar but they are never quite warm enough. The Ring-tailed Lemur or Madagascar Cat [1] is caught by sailors who have enough Parrots already. The Gentle Lemur is devoted to his human keeper and often bites him severely. The Aye-aye has large movable ears caused by listening for Grubs. The Potto is rather peevish. The Spectral Tarsier of the West Indies is uncanny. He has huge bug-eyes, elongated ankles and knobby toes. He is sometimes confused with Delirium Tremens. Lemurs comb their hair with their lower front teeth. They mature almost instantaneously. In a way we came from Lemurs because they are also descended from an extinct Tree Shrew something like a large Rat. From the Tree Shrew to the Dogfish is but a step, which practically brings us to the Amœba. So perhaps the Lemur is to blame for it all.[2]

[1] *Lemur catta.*
[2] Aristotle would not have known a Lemur if it came up and bit him. He had enough to keep track of, without Lemurs.

WHAT I HATE ABOUT SPRING

*

I AM not an ornithologist, whatever people may say. I could look Sigmund Freud himself in the face and make that statement without batting an eye. Still, I know what I know.

Ornithologists are all right—I'm only saying that I'm not one. As a rule they are very nice old gentlemen, indeed, and they don't mind lying a blue streak about their little pets, either. I like that. If I am ever accused of ruining the crops I certainly want an ornithologist to defend me.

I know that for many of my fellow creatures existence without our Feathered Friends would be a living hell. I guess I'm just different.

If, in his meanderings through field and wood, one of these persons encounters a Pewee, it thrills him through and through. It really does. For him that day is a red-letter day, a day of days, instinct with something sacred and beautiful that no one, come

(47)

what may, can ever take away. Personally, whenever I meet one of the darn things I can say and do all that is needful in the time it takes me to pick up a brick.

Maybe I shouldn't confess it, but a Pewee means just about nothing to me, unless he is peeping and pipping beyond all human endurance. A Pewee in a state of comparative quiescence is only a Pewee to me, if that. Should I be in a thinking mood when I see him, I may recall that he is notoriously peppered with parasites; he stirs within me no deeper philosophic vein. I draw my overalls aside and hasten by. I'm really not the Pewee type—a fact upon which I have always rather prided myself.

Please don't misunderstand. I'm not against all the birds. Let us have birds, by all means, but in some sort of moderation. I am not suggesting a general massacre of the feathered tribe; not at present. The times are not ripe for so drastic a move, and I'm not at all sure I'd approve, anyway. If this book breathes anything at all, and I assure you there have been moments during its composition—but we needn't go into that; it breathes, I was going to say, the spirit of toleration. Let's grin and bear it.

I sincerely hope that all birds are not like the Jones's Island birds. There must be some splendid ones, or else they have shown only the better side of their nature to such authors as the late Mr. Audubon, Mr. Thoreau and Mr. Burroughs. I write, more in sorrow than in anger, as one who has heard them at their worst. As species the birds of Jones's may be unexceptionable; as individuals they leave much to be desired. Somehow the rowdy element has got in.

Messrs. Audubon, Thoreau and Burroughs were surely within their rights in penning their excellent volumes, but I can't help feeling that they encouraged certain unfortunate tendencies. And, by the way, I do not consider myself nearly so good a writer as any two of them. One thing I will say in their favor, they knew a bird when they saw it and could tell you its name. Myself, I have never been able to find out which bird belongs to which noise. I only know that some are much worse.

I only know that summer and summer, spring after ear-splitting spring, my continuous efforts to concentrate against an infinity of birds are beginning to take their toll. That's why I'm making a stand.

Indeed, evolution is now staging one of its interesting demonstrations right here on my sandbar, with me and the birdies as Exhibits A and B. I fancy the birdies will survive. They have no living to make. I don't bother them a bit. And it is extremely doubtful that I can continue to function as a book reviewer while being hooted, whistled, squawked, trilled and cadenzaed at for twenty-three hours out of the twenty-four. Some mornings it is possible to snatch a few winks of troubled sleep; but mostly I lie awake, listening, willy-nilly, to the rapturous cries issuing from thousands, nay, millions, of ecstatic throats. This proves that their sex life is O. K. Well, that's just fine for them.

Ah, me! I suppose it's all my fault—yes, it is!

(49)

More than one psychologist has hinted that there must be something amiss with a bookish old recluse who does not enjoy the combined yawpings and yowlings and yammerings of the entire brute creation while he is trying to get some plain and fancy writing done. I reply that there must be something wrong, and radically wrong, with a lot of birds who cannot let a poor hack have five minutes of peace in which to grind out his copy.

I advise pedants to skip my classification of bird noises. I find that most birds, if left to their own devices, are likely to go *zeegle zeegle zeegle*. There is also the *bloop* type, and I may as well mention the *phut phut* and *willuch willuch* varieties—see the text of my articles for the details.

Or, one may divide the avifauna of Jones's into those that sound like scraping a blackboard with chalk, those that resemble the sound produced by blowing into a bunghole, and those that remind the hearer of delicate steel gimlets boring remorsely into the more sensitive tissues of the human brain. Another bird which I should love to get my hands on emits a circular whiz guaranteed to turn a cave-man into an incurable neurotic in five minutes of steady application. Perhaps I may be pardoned for regarding the Jones's Island Whizzer as a menace to American letters.

So far I have been unable to obtain specimens for study. Always by the time I have dropped everything, including my career, seized the poker and arrived at the center of disturbance, some low form of cunning has enabled the musicians to get away and resume operations just out of reach. Malicious animal magnetism bothers them not one bit. They eat it up. It seems to inspire them.

Large numbers of the Jones's Island birds owe their present health to protective coloration. But I do believe I got a Chippy squarely on the beak with a clam-shell the other day.

I am inclined to think, after consulting my bird guide and common sense, that the thing that yelps on my clothes-pole at regular intervals during the night is a Great Bustard. Sometimes it brings a Little Bustard along. I have noticed no signs of a Rhinoceros Auklet about, and a very good thing for it, too.

There are, moreover, no Nightingales here, God forbid, or I might more fully savor the gentle Elia's remark to Wordsworth, "If I am kept from sleep, I do not see much difference between Nightingales and Cats." In my opinion the Cat never mewed that could equal a Lesser Scaup, let alone a Nightingale, at in-ducing a horror of all natural phenomena.

The Nightingale hasn't come to America yet, but mark my words, it will. Somebody will bring it. I cannot trust myself to speak more freely or at length about the Nightingale. I might say something I'd regret.

Sometimes I think we have Bobolinks. There is an animal I cannot mention calmly. I attribute many of the misfortunes of after life to the fact that I once had to speak "Robert of Lincoln" in school, "Spink, spank, spink" and all. You cannot live down a thing like that. Others may not know it, but you do. Naturally, I regard "Spink, spank, spink" as the worst single line in or out of poetry, unless it is "Chee, chee, chee." A close runner-up is that "Cuckoo, jug-jug, tu-whee, to-whitta whoo" thing. I will leave it to any fair-minded jury whether the man who wrote that was drunk or sober.

Meanwhile I am going to try to think more kindly of the birds. They are not entirely to blame. You know they used to be reptiles, and that really explains a great deal. The next time a Chipping Sparrow bursts impolitely into an aria while I am on the track of my predicate, I'm going to count ten and mutter, "Well, what can you expect? It's only a modified reptile!"

RETURN OF THE BIRDS

*

THE ROBIN

THE WREN

THE CUCKOO

THE BOOBY

THE NIGHTINGALE

THE CROW

THE STORK

THE ROBIN

THE Robin is called the harbinger of spring because he makes so much noise. He starts singing under your window before daylight in March and continues with brief intermissions for lunch until you are taken to Bellevue. The Robin is cheerful. His message consists of *cheerily cheerily cheerily cheer-up* repeated in a loud hearty voice *ad libitum* and slightly off key.

In our language this means that all is for the best and that it pays to smile and that kind words are more than coronets and that God is love.[1] The Robin often survives our Northern winters and brickbats.[2] The Robin helps the crops because he destroys the noxious insects such as Japanese Beetles, sponge cake and cherries. This is a very cute habit unless you raise cherries. If the Robin were larger he would be stealing prunes in the chain stores and the Baumes Law would get him. As it is nothing much can be done. The Robin has a brilliant vest. The female is somewhat duller. The Robin hops after the gardener, picking up earthworms and freshly sown seeds. He knows so many cute little tricks that sometimes he seems almost human and that is about all we can say of our nearest and dearest. Robins migrate,[3] so those who dislike them can migrate in the opposite direction. Certain parts of the Sahara Desert are said to be free from Robins for several weeks each year.[4]

[1] The Robin's call, as distinguished from his song, is *pip pip* or *tsee tsee* or *gloop gloop*. This is said to mean either "Hip, hip, hooray, boys, spring is here!" or "Oh, how I wish I had another worm!"

[2] They manage these things better in Italy. One of the joys of motoring through the Abruzzi is the chance of joining the local Robin militia in a *safari* and participating afterwards in a steaming bowl of *Merli alla cacciatore con polenta* or Robin country style with a dash of garlic.

[3] Robins appear to be responsible for an interesting nervous affliction, in which the victim believes that any Robin he sees is the same Robin he saw last spring and that the bird returned from winter quarters especially to visit him. This may go on for years.

[4] The Robin cocks his head and looks at you, but you never know what he thinks. This may be just as well.

THE WREN

THE Wren is a very affectionate bird. He loves us for ourself alone and not because we provide him with room and board. You can prove that a Wren loves you by forcing his paws around your neck, laying his head on your shoulder, and repeating "Oh, how he loves me!" If he bites you try another Wren. Wrens lead immoral lives. Statistics show that 99 3-5 per cent of them are sexually promiscuous [1] and otherwise emotionally unbalanced. Indeed, the practice of bird-banding has revealed social conditions among Wrens closely resembling those preceding the Fall of Rome and following the late World War. Wrens are encouraged by nice old ladies who think they are doing good. The Wren-box problem is becoming more acute each year, for Wrens now demand better housing conditions, labor-saving devices and shorter hours. The Wren has a stubby tail and a vicious expression. His sweet bubbling song means that he has just punctured the eggs of a Chipping Sparrow and ruined the home of a Yellow Warbler and is going out to murder a couple of baby Titmice.[2] Jenny Wren feeds her young 971 times each day so that they will grow up and be like father. In ordinary conversation Wrens go *plit plit, cheep cheep* and *whee-udel whee-udel whee-udel.* The way to have Wrens is to wish for a Bluebird. Then you'll have plenty.

[1] This does not apply to English Wrens, for Viscount Grey of Fallodon assures us, "British birds are monogamous; this is the rule, and the exceptions are few." Viscount Grey's exceptions are the Cuckoo, the Ruff and Reeve, the Capercaillie and Black Game. But English Wrens are troglodytes and you know what they are.

[2] On the other hand, a Wren living near a Mr. Innes of Bandrakehead, in the parish of Colton, Westmoreland, adopted and reared two infant Titmice orphaned by a cruel sportsman in June, 1835, caring for them with the utmost assiduity. We owe these facts to a clergyman who had a gift for seeing the most extraordinary things and sticking to them.

THE CUCKOO

CUCKOOS have been known from the remotest times and they are still going strong. Cuckoos lack all sense of responsibility. They lay their eggs in other birds' nests [1] and devote their entire attention to matters of which the less said the better. The female Cuckoo is polyandrous and the male has zygodactylous feet. They do exactly as they please and if some other bird tries to stop them they fly away and do it somewhere else. The young Cuckoos are hatched and reared by Dunnocks,[2] Meadow Pipits, Titlarks and Wagtails, whose rightful progeny they eject from the nest in order to get all the worms.[3] The call of the Yellow-billed Cuckoo of North America is often mistaken for a Bloodhound drinking a bowl of milk. He goes *cowlp cowlp cowlp*. The Great Spotted Cuckoo of the Himalayas goes *kark kark* or *burroo burroo* or *orange pekoe, orange pekoe*. Cuckoos never marry.[4] Cuckoos may seem crazy but when you realize that each one consumes eight hundred Woolly Caterpillars a day do you wonder? [5] Cuckoos migrate but not nearly enough. Cuckoos are a Godsend to authors. The only way to stop writing about Cuckoos is simply to stop.[6]

[1] Some say that the female Cuckoo lays her egg on the ground and conveys it to the nest of her dupe by means of the bill. This phenomenon is said to have been witnessed by two Scottish lads, sons of a Mr. Tripeny, a farmer in Coxmuir, on June 24th, 1838, and later by Adolf Müller, a forester of Gladenbach, in Darmstadt, who saw the whole thing through a telescope.

[2] The Dunnock is nothing but the Hedge Sparrow, which is not a Sparrow at all, but a kind of Thrush. As I write this note I have failed to discover what a Meadow Pipit really is. I mention these things merely to show what I have been through in writing this book.

[3] American Cuckoos do none of these awful things. They marry, own their own homes and bring up their own Cuckoos. But they are still Cuckoos.

[4] When questioned closely about their hatred of home life, Cuckoos shrug and say that they know what they know—always an extremely dubious assertion.

[5] One of the essentials of Cuckoo study is always to bear in mind that you are dealing with Cuckoos. For instance, what might seem decidedly off-color or even reprehensible in a Pouter Pigeon is perfectly all right for a Cuckoo. Here is a field for our much vaunted modern tolerance. Did they ask to be Cuckoos?

[6] Why the poets, especially, should find Cuckoos so congenial a subject I have no idea. That is to say, if I had an idea I should not dream of making it public.

THE BOOBY

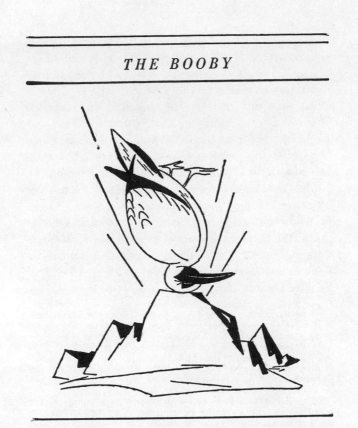

THE Booby is something like a Goose. He builds his nest on a cliff and eats Flying Fishes, Herrings and Squids. His favorite sport is diving from a great height onto a rock which he believes to be a delicious bit of sea-food. After each dive there is one less Booby. The Booby is thrifty. He hoards his provisions, which are then stolen by the Frigate Bird. The

Blue-faced Booby, so called from his reddish feet, is sometimes found in California. Other Boobies have blackish, brownish, greenish or purplish feet and inhabit various parts of the British Empire. The sun never sets on the Booby. They breed in vast numbers. When first approaching the mating grounds the Booby flies sixty miles an hour because he expects to be happy for life as soon as he gets there.[1] The male helps hatch the eggs and sometimes he is sorry he did. He has that much sense. Young Boobies are not unattractive but they grow up. Boobies float out to sea in flocks but they never get lost.[2] Fossil remains show that there have always been Boobies. If there were no Boobies it would be necessary to invent them. Boobies quack, grunt and whistle. Heine said he loved Boobies because they were such good copy.[3]

[1] I do not believe in disabusing young Boobies of this notion. If it helps them to be happy for a couple of weeks, isn't it all to the good?

[2] Quite naturally, they associate with the Noddies, such as the Common Noddy, the Lesser Noddy, the White-capped Noddy, the Blue-grey Noddy and the Hawaiian Noddy. The Common Noddy is much smaller than the Booby. The Lesser Noddy is very much smaller.

[3] The Booby is a kind of Gannet, sometimes known as the Solan Goose, and is not to be confused with Lewis Gannett, the handsome critic, editorial writer, man about town and *raconteur* of the *New York Herald Tribune.* The author carefully left this information out of his article for fear it might get people to thinking. Lewis disapproved of this procedure on the ground that people may have been thinking already. I still believe there is no cause for alarm. Mr. Gannett's name is spelled with two *t*s.

THE NIGHTINGALE

THE Nightingale is a familiar figure in poems beginning "Oh, Nightingale!" all based on other poems beginning "Oh, Nightingale!" The Nightingale is famous for singing all night as well as all day. He sings in the middle of hedgerows and spinneys where nothing can hit him. He is much loved by persons who are slightly deaf. The Nightingale is called the greatest of our feathered songsters because he is no better than the Hermit Thrush, the Skylark, the Robin, the Bullfinch, the Orchard Oriole, the Blue-capped Motmot of Brazil and the Tawny-shouldered Podargus of Australia. The Nightingale goes *zo zo zo zo, ze ze ze ze* and *jug jug jug jug terea*, like parts of Beethoven's "Pastoral Symphony." Untutored auditors have compared these sounds to a creaking axle, two creaking axles, an ailing pump handle and just plain squawks.[1] The Nightingale sings with the syrinx. The larynx isn't good enough. The psychology of the Nightingale has been much misunderstood. He does not sing to impress his wife, who remains in the nest with her ears tucked under her wing, trying to forget. He is training for the annual visit to the British Empire Naturalists' Association and his radio public. He is wound up until the fifteenth of June and nothing can stop him excepting a charge of No. 10 shot. The plumage is the same in both sexes, as so often occurs among musical birds. The Nightingale teaches that there is always something. If you had everything that money could buy there would still be the Nightingale.[2]

[1] Agrippina, the mother of Nero, had an Albino Nightingale, and I have often thought that this might explain a few things about Nero—no special things, just things in general. At any rate, Nero became an enthusiastic bird-lover.

[2] A Scots farmer, after a visit to the South of England, is said to have remarked, "I wadna gie the wheeple o' a whaup for a' the Nightingales that ever whooped." The Nightingale is not encouraged in Scotland and Wales (excepting in Glamorganshire, where there is a colony of nature-lovers). He enters Ireland at his own risk.

THE CROW

THE Crow is tough. He uses no baby talk even in mating season. During courtship the male feeds the female but he soon gets wise to himself. He does not help incubate. He thinks he's done enough. Married Crows spend their time fighting because they are birds of a feather. The Crow pulls up the corn, ruins the lettuce, pecks at the hired man's eyes, kidnaps young Chickens, scatters poison ivy and disseminates

the germs of Hog cholera, roup and bumble-foot. For
these reasons he is called the farmer's friend. Crows
bathe when it rains. Their nests are lined with Rabbit
fur. The Raven is called Ralph or Grip.[1] Crows hold
courts of justice where sentence is passed upon Crows
who do not know the mayor. After much cawing by
the judge and a jury of the usual sort the defendant
is torn to pieces to teach him a lesson. All and sundry
then repair to a nearby tree to commit simony, petty
larceny, tergiversation and misfeasance, evict a few
widows and orphans, double-cross one another and
make more laws. After a good laugh they hold evening
prayers and go to roost in the wrong nests. Aristotle
described the Crow as chaste. In some departments of
knowledge Aristotle was too innocent for his own
good. I am frequently asked the meaning of *Caw!
Caw! Caw!* [2] It means nothing whatever.

[1] If you cannot distinguish between the various members of
the Crow family, don't let it worry you. Good livings have
been made by telling anecdotes designed to show the great
intelligence of the Raven, the Rook, the Jackdaw, the Chough
and the Magpie, but the field is overcrowded at present. For
obvious reasons Crows seem more intelligent to some people
than to others.

[2] These are stirring times for Crow commentators, who are
beginning to wonder if the Crow really does say *Caw! Caw!
Caw!* Some of the young moderns hold that the bird says
Caar! Caar! Caar! and others insist upon *Karrr! Karrr! Kaar!*
Indeed, one courageous scholar has come out for *Varawk!
Verawk! Varawk!* The fact is, it depends entirely upon the
individual Crow.

THE STORK

THE Stork is a sad looking bird with a strange sense of humor. He is fond of practical jokes. The Stork stands on one leg holding in his bill the ends of a large napkin containing guess what. He rests his bill on his chest while thinking up more fun. He has a supratemporal fenestra or vacuity. Storks nest on chimney-tops. They are said to bring good luck to the household but some households do not need any more luck. It isn't the Stork so much, it's the upkeep. They return year after year to the same chimney if the family is dumb enough. Some Storks can be trained to nest on neighboring chimneys but they always come back. The word "Shoo!" means nothing to a Stork. The Stork gets into the subway and even goes up in airplanes. He has been seen under gooseberry bushes. The Stork knows everything. He is found in all countries, especially on the East Side of New York. The Black Stork is a native of Africa.[1] The ancients regarded the Stork as a symbol of conjugal fidelity, farm relief, membranous croup and grocery bills.[2] The Stork is voiceless because there is really nothing to say. He makes a snapping sound with his bill which is said to denote mirth. It is against the law to tell you any more about the Stork.

[1] The Wood Stork is not so well known because he minds his own business.
[2] The Stork was held in veneration by the Thessalonians. His annual arrival was greeted with great rejoicing by the male inhabitants. Thessalonians were something like Mormons.

PERFECTLY DAMNABLE BIRDS

*

THE GREAT BUSTARD

THE OWL

THE LOVE BIRD

THE HEN

THE ROOSTER

THE CANARY

THE Great Bustard (from the Greek *Bustard,* meaning Bustard) inhabits foreign countries such as Turkestan, Southern Siberia and Mesopotamia. Great Bustards are occasionally observed in Great Britain where they are said to have become extinct in 1838.[1] They are apt to become extinct almost anywhere because they are so wary that they leave the nest at sight of a stranger and let their eggs addle.[2] There have never been any Bustards in the good old U. S. A. Bustards are ugly brown birds something like Turkeys. They are fond of turnips, parsnips, cereals, Mice, myriapods and mimosa gum. They spend their time being Bustards. They do not like to be called Bustards but that is what they are just the same. Their love life is rather distressing. The male Bustard possesses a large sublingual pouch or gular sac which he uses to attract the female Bustard in some manner best known to Bustards. When he sees a female he inflates this object, turns himself practically inside out and struts around uttering booming or crooning sounds resembling *prunt prunt*.[3] She does not know that he has a schizognathous palate and a tracheo-bronchial syrinx, that his metatarsus is covered with reticulated scales and that he completely lacks the ectipicondylar process on the outer side of the lower end of the humerus. The Little Bustard is worse, if anything. The Little Bustard can be tamed just before Christmas. There are forty different kinds of Bustards.

[1] The last of the British Bustards were several old hens living in the neighborhood of Swaffham in Norfolk. There were no males anywhere near. Some ornithologists believe that the poor hens finally did away with themselves. It is quite possible, however, that they knew what they were doing.

[2] It has been the author's experience that birds so wary as all that seldom have anything of a constructive nature to offer. Beautiful birds are always more reasonable, perhaps because they are used to being chased. They understand why and all about it. Ugly birds never understand anything.

[3] Statistics show that exhibitionists do not always make ideal husbands, since they are likely to keep right on with the habit, and not at home, either. I don't say that all exhibitionists are like that, but some of them are. The female should have thought of this, but you know how it is.

THE OWL

THE Owl has been called the Bird of Wisdom because he is so solemn. He cannot see a joke
because he lacks certain portions of the cerebrum or
forebrain.[1] He looks you through and through as
though he knew your entire past but he is only going
by hearsay.[2] The Owl does not have much fun. He
has a shallow symphisis and a rudimentary aftershaft
and his basal cere is sparsely feathered. But he can
expand and contract his iris and his two outer toes

are reversible. Owls eat Rats, Mice,[3] Voles, Lemmings, Grouse and Koalas. Many kind-hearted persons have spent years giving sugar to Owls. Owls do not like sugar. The mating call of the Screech Owl [4] is said to remind the wicked of Judgment Day.[5] The Hoot Owl goes *Whoo-whoo-whoo Wh-whoo to-whoo-ah* and the Tawny or Shakespearean Owl goes *tu-whit to-who* and the Barn or Monkey-faced Owl [6] goes *geep geep.* The Great Horned Owl [7] passes the day in dark forests, old church towers and graveyards planning ways to scare us all silly. If you do not like these birds you can go to the North Pole where you will find the Snowy Owl, the meanest of the whole family. Owls [8] teach us to keep our hands out of hollow trees.

[1] Quite sensibly, the Owl regards his infirmity as a signal merit. He is responsible for the widespread belief that the highest form of intelligence consists principally in not being able to see a joke. Isn't that just like an Owl?

[2] This appears to be a safe statement, since stuffed Owls look at you in exactly the same way, and *they* can't be psychoanalyzing you! Or can they?

[3] Owls kill vast numbers of Mice, but most people would rather have the Mice. Mice contain Vitamins A, B and G.

[4] There is perhaps nothing more nerve-racking on earth, unless it is parts of *Tristan und Isolde.*

[5] The Screech Owl makes a most amusing pet. The bird flies at visitors and buries its talons in their scalps, sometimes causing them to break a leg in their headlong flight, to the accompaniment of gales of laughter from the owners. After a mass meeting of neighbors, the bird sometimes disappears as suddenly as it came. The owners often disappear, too.

[6] The way Barn Owls conduct themselves, you can hardly get anybody to go into a Barn with you any more.

[7] Pliny tells us that a Horned Owl entered the sanctuary of the Capitol in the consulship of Palepius and Padanius, in consequence of which Rome was purified on the Nones of March in that year. Then everything was all right again.

[8] The female Owl is so awful that she deserves a whole book to herself. Owlishness is so foreign to the truly feminine nature that when it does occur it is simply appalling. In males one expects a certain amount of it.

THE LOVE BIRD

THE Love Bird or Connubial Parakeet is one hundred per cent faithful to his mate who is locked into the same cage. They sit close together on the perch, partly to keep warm [1] and partly for want of something better to do. [2] If anyone is around, the male Love Bird twitters sweetly into the ear of his mate, who responds in kind, sometimes adding a furtive peck in the posterior mandibular process. When they think they are unobserved they kick each other off the perch and sit in opposite corners making horrible faces and insulting remarks. They are known to insiders as the most pugnacious of all birds.[3] During adolescence and nidification Love Birds talk baby talk. The female will believe anything. The brain of the male Love Bird weighs two milligrams more than his mate's but the female is better at nagging. They breed readily in confinement, almost too readily. Strangely enough Love Birds have no merrythought or furcula. Both sexes spend a good deal of time in molting [4] and the female complains of draughts. None of this helps in the home. The Blue-rumped Love Bird of Namaqualand is a little too much. If anything happens to one of the pair the other instantly expires of inconsolable grief. Now you tell one.[5]

[1] They are tropical birds and can hardly be expected to act like Arctic Three-toed Woodpeckers, who thrive on twin perches.

[2] Naturally, they tend to run out of ideas; that is, new ideas.

[3] A correspondent of Mr. W. T. Greene writes of one of his Love Birds that "a more surly, ill-tempered little glutton never existed." To one's complete surprise he means the female, for he adds: "She quarrels with her husband, whom she drives about, compels to feed her and then thrashes if he does not sit closely enough to her on the perch." The postscript is even more astonishing: "And yet he seems to like it and to be specially proud of his beautiful but utterly unamiable wife."

[4] Certain birds, notably the Pipit, the Wagtail and the Penguin, molt more than seems at all necessary. There are the postnatal, the postjuvenal, the prenuptial and the postnuptial molts. It is difficult to say which is the worst.

[5] No useful purpose would be served by running on about this animal. Whole libraries have been written on the Love Bird and much good it has done. Besides, the subject is very difficult. There seems to be a catch in it somewhere.

THE HEN

THE Hen or female Chicken is an essential part of Chicken farming, one of the major psychoses.[1] The Hen has no business sense. She lays very poorly when eggs are expensive. At other times you can't stop her. Hens cluck a lot. The Hen says *tuk tuk tuk tuk twork*. The more disillusioned Hens say merely *twork*. When a Hen says nothing but *twork* [2] she has seen her best days. Hens have no teeth and are easily hypnotized. Some Hens are more attractive than others. The Plymouth Rock is a good all-around Hen. She is willing to lay or sit or be fried because it is all the same to her. But her many virtues pall in time. She becomes more and more Henlike. Old Plymouth Rocks should be boiled. If you have been around Plymouth Rocks almost any other Hen seems wonderful. The White Leghorn is perfectly grand [3] and Rhode Island Reds are all right for a change. The Hen is very patient. She does not seem to mind. The Hen exhibits a touching devotion to her home. She has been known to starve rather than abandon a nestful of glass eggs or old doorknobs. She cares for her Chicks all day long, providing them with food and bad advice and frequently trampling them flat. The Chick's aim in life is to wander into the shrubbery and get lost and fall into a pan of water. This is called instinct. Nowadays many Chicks are born in incubators. They spend their formative period in parcels post containers.[4]

[1] A net profit of $186,293.00 has been realized in this business on an initial outlay of $5.77, including $0.50 for the Hen, $0.27 for the eggs and $5.00 for the cocaine.

[2] *Twork* is capable of an almost infinite number of inflections and meanings. It probably covers the whole ground.

[3] The White Leghorn is a Mediterranean or non-sitting variety. She is a bad mother, but she is so pretty that it doesn't matter. Sitting is not the whole of life by any means.

[4] The effect upon their general outlook may be imagined. Incubator Chicks eagerly snatch and swallow red worsted Worms fed to them by professors of biology. This proves several things about all concerned.

THE ROOSTER

THE Rooster is rather conceited and so would you be. He is a bad example to the young and also to the old because he is noisy, impertinent, contumacious and fond of spring onions. He has been called the Bird of Morn because he spoils the whole morning with his frightful yells. He is not mentioned in the Old Testament. The clarion cry of the Rooster is one of Nature's devices for increasing nervous prostration. The Rooster wakes up and crows at 2 A.M., a habit variously attributed to peculiarities of the epiglottis, original sin and pure meanness. It is probable that the crowing of the ancestral Rooster or Bankiva Jungle Fowl of India accounts for the widespread desire for Nirvana among the Hindus as well as the practice of Suttee. There are people who like it. The Rooster has wattles and hackles.[1] His brain occupies an empty space near the sinciput. The Rooster is a medium husband and father. In defense of his loved ones he will often attack a fullgrown Grasshopper, Spider or Fly. Besides, he makes the sun rise. The Rooster has no ideal Hen. When his wife hatches Ducklings he is jealous. He jumps to conclusions. The Rooster is not really wicked or vicious.[2] It's just his way. It is not true that Roosters are all alike. The Dorkings are fine old birds but they have extra toes and are very unhappy. The Buff Orpingtons (of the Lincolnshire Buff Orpingtons) [3] are somewhat pretentious. They claim the right to be eaten by royalty. Light Brahmas are handsome enough but they have ankle fluff. Bantams are not worth talking about.[4]

[1] Aristotle wondered about the composition of the Rooster's comb. He says that "whereas it is not just exactly flesh, at the same time it is not easy to say what else it is." Aristotle had never heard of cellophane.

[2] A Rooster who laid an egg in the town of Bâle, Switzerland, in 1474, was tried for witchcraft, convicted and publicly burnt; and serve him right. Too much of that sort of thing would never do.

[3] Reginald Buff Orpington actually succeeded in being eaten by royalty in Jubilee Year. For all their airs, however, the Buff Orpingtons are nothing but a local cross of Cochin and Dorking. They are unrelated to the Black Orpingtons, who derive from the Langshans.

[4] The Capon does not crow. Why should he?

THE CANARY

THE Canary gives pleasure to many persons who would otherwise get very little. The song of the Canary has inspired numerous poems, acts of heroism and outbreaks of homicidal mania.[1] It is the female Mosquito that bites but it is the male Canary that sings.[2] Canaries have the pip, asthma, apthæ and inflammation of the syrinx. They should be treated with borax, glycerin, turpentine, alum, infusions of quassia, tincture of lobelia, syrup of squills and a paste made of equal parts of hard-boiled egg, crackers and potassium cyanide. Canaries are used to detect the presence of deadly gas in mines but there are not enough mines to go round. Other Canary problems can be solved with the assistance of a skilled taxidermist. Canaries are very prolific, to put it that way.[3] One pair could have 25,000,000,000 descendants in several years but they do not seem to do so. Dark brown males mate with light green females. Light yellow females mate with Siskins, Chaffinches and Bullfinches of any color. The offspring are called hybrids or Mules.[4] If you have a Canary you brought it on yourself, didn't you?[5]

[1] The tendency of Canary owners and their neighbors to peculiar mental states need not be taken too seriously. After all, as some philosopher has observed, one might as well go mad one way as the other.

[2] A hardened cynic was once heard to mutter, "The more I hear of Canaries the better I like Cats." When his wife insisted upon having a Canary, he went out and bought her a female.

[3] In "The Bird Fancier's Companion," under the caption, "Breeding," I find: "This is a very important item, as well as amusing." I can see how the breeding of Canaries might be important, but why amusing? I fear there will never be anything approaching a general agreement about what is funny and what isn't.

[4] After years of patient effort the head-masters of Canary schools have succeeded in producing several types which look and act like practically anything but Canaries. These birds regard ordinary Harz Mountain Canaries as social nonentities or "untouchables." The Belgians do a great deal of this sort of thing when they are not occupied with Hares.

[5] The Canary was introduced into Europe in the sixteenth century, when a vessel containing some of them was wrecked on the Coast of Italy. The little songsters immediately spread over the whole civilized world. This has been called one of the tragedies of the sea. In the year 1871 no less than 60,000 Canaries were brought to the United States. Of this number 59,000 were named Dick.

BIRDS I COULD DO WITHOUT

*

THE PEWEE

THE COMMON BABBLER

THE NUTHATCH

THE LOON

THE WATER OUZEL

THE FLAMINGO

THE PEWEE

THE Pewee is famous for catching Flies and going *pee-a-wee pee-a-wee* all day long. His melancholy call is greatly enjoyed by those who enjoy that sort of thing.[1] Others find it extremely depressing. The Pewee is easy to identify. If it isn't anything else especially it's a Pewee. The sexes are alike in most ways. The Pewee is very lucky because all he needs to be happy is another nice fresh insect.[2] He believes that he is Napoleon. The Pewee is incompetent, irrelevant and immaterial.[3] The Phoebe or Porch Pewee is often called the Dear Little Phoebe. She builds her nest out of new moss so that it will not be noticed when placed on a bright red porch. She is very friendly and is covered with parasites.[4] Phoebes twitch their tails and go *phoe-be phoe-be*. The larger Flycatchers [5] are very ill-natured and disagreeable birds. They have bristles around the bill and their young are mottled. During the mating season they utter continuous low shrieks. This is caused by love. The Chebec or Least Flycatcher subsists upon Gnats and Midges. He goes *chebec chebec* or *toora-loora-loo*. He is very immoral but it doesn't matter because the whole bird is only five and a half inches long.

[1] Henry D. Thoreau heard a Pewee singing on May 22nd, 1854, and again on the following day (May 23rd, 1854). He found two nests on June 27th, 1858, and took them home on August 13th of the same year. He saw some Ducks on April 1st, 1853, and on December 4th, 1856, his Cat caught a Mouse.

[2] What the Pewee achieves in this way may or not be happiness in the best and truest sense, but if it seems so to him it probably amounts to the same thing.

[3] For once we agree with John Burroughs, who couldn't abide Pewees. He considered that "no birds are so little calculated to excite pleasurable emotion in the beholder, or to become objects of human interest and affection." In later life Burroughs became reconciled to Pewees.

[4] It is great fun to watch a big, hulking bird-lover fleeing from a bevy of Dear Little Phoebes upon learning about the parasites, generally after having attributed this and that to some entirely different agency. There is no use trying to desert a Phoebe once you have adopted her. All you can do is lay in a supply of Black Flag and get what you can out of life.

[5] There used to be talk of turning the marked talents of these birds to some useful end, such as catching Flies indoors, but nothing ever came of it. They still destroy millions of the little pests where it does not the slightest good. Meanwhile the Fly problem remains about where it was, like all the problems,

THE Common Babbler is found in Afghanistan and Baluchistan although the inhabitants of both countries deny it. Sometimes the Afghans succeed in hanging it on the Baluches and *vice versa*. This is largely to blame for the worried discouraged appearance of Afghans and Baluches. Common Babblers bustle about in groups under the wild caper bushes, turning over dead leaves and making low remarks. Authorities differ on what Common Babblers are trying to get off their epigastriums. To the layman it

(87)

sounds like *blatt blatt* or *clack clack* or *gabble gabble gabble* or *jabber jabber jabber* [1] and probably means that the Yellow-eyed Babbler of India, Burma and Siam is no better than she should be because she has a rufous back, orange eyebrows and an albescent abdomen.[2] Babblers often stop in front of automobiles to babble but something seems to protect them. There are also male Common Babblers. Both sexes are very untidy. Common Babblers [3] will never become extinct because they mate in March, April, May, June, July, August, September, October, November, December, January and February. After a visit to Afghanistan or Baluchistan it is great to get back to the Long-tailed Chat, the Long-winded Chiff-chaff, the Whooping Crane, the Perpetual Warbler, the Screech Owl and the Aspirin.

[1] A combination of all these sounds, with the addition of *klunk klunk* and *whee-ee-ee*, will give you a rough idea of conditions in the Near East.

[2] The upper plumage of the Common Babbler is fulvous-brown, the chin is fulvous-white and the lower feathers are just fulvous. In fact, the Common Babbler is one of our most fulvous birds. Fulvous birds do not like rufous or plumbeous birds.

[3] The White-headed Babbler is a familiar sight to anyone who has ever been in Ceylon, and who hasn't? Or perhaps I should ask, who has? The Spotted Babbler of Cochin-China is something else again.

THE NUTHATCH

THE Nuthatch cannot sing and does not try. He belongs on the Honor Roll of Songless Birds with the Stork, the Cedar Waxwing, the Pie-faced Anhinga and a Robin I met the other day. He says *yank yank* and *nyaa nyaa* and *cmfwpp cmfwpp* and lets it go at that.[1] The Nuthatch is often mistaken for the Philadelphia Vireo because some people at best are not very bright.[2] He has been called the Upside

Down Bird because he creeps headfirst down the trunks of trees.[3] How he gets back is another story. There is never a cross word in a Nuthatch home because they are both too busy placing nuts in crevices and cracking them with their beaks. Nuthatches chum with Chickadees, Downy Woodpeckers and Brown Creepers. They all go looking for sunflower seeds, bits of chopped suet and sugar. Nuthatches have solved the problem of hospitality. They place pitch around the front door so that nobody comes. The word *Nuthatch* is believed to be a combination of the words *nut* and *hatch*. Nuthatches do not hatch nuts, but supposing they did?

[1] A leading authority asserts of the Nuthatch's call: "The tone is a clear falsetto, best imitated by pinching the nose and singing the note *staccato,* with as much of the nasal quality as one can put into it." If my readers really want to please me, they will not do this.

[2] Color-blindness also complicates the subject. Color-blind persons cannot tell the Red-breasted Nuthatch from the Indigo Bunting, the Pink-footed Shearwater, the Green Bee-eater, the Coffee-bellied Puffleg of Bogata, the Purple-rumped Sunbird of Patagonia and the Blue-whiskered Bulbul of the Himalayas. You will notice that the birds have few secrets from the busy scientist.

[3] Nuthatches really prefer this method of locomotion. They do not seem to be dizzy. It may be that they are dizzy and do not know it, or that they are dizzy and know it but do not know why, or that they are dizzy and like it, or so on. How they came to be upside down in the first place need not concern us. It isn't our fault, at any rate.

THE LOON

THE Loon bobs up in the surf on dark nights, ruins your summer with a burst of wild maniacal laughter, then dives and waits for the next victim. And he wonders why people shoot at him. The Loon's conversation consists of *Wah-hoo-oo-o* and *Oh-ha-ha-ha-ha* and *Haw! Haw! Haw! Haw! Haw!* He could not do without his sense of humor but we could.[1] The cry of the Loon is said to portend rain or a long dry spell.[2] Loons marry for better or worse, chiefly the latter. They have red eyes and can hold their breath for eight minutes. The male Loon indulges in amorous frolics in the water and often meets with an enthusiastic response. They are practically helpless on land. Loons cannot rise from the water except against the wind. When becalmed they fall asleep and drift about on the waves until they bump into something. This also strikes them as funny. Loons resemble large Grebes but are less Grebelike.[3] These birds are easy to tell apart because the Loon has a flat metatarsus while the Grebe has a Y-shaped furcula and a membranous hallux. The hind toe of the Little Grebe or Dabchick is scalloped. All the diving birds are slightly mad. Our only hope at present seems to lie in eugenics because if you tried to educate a Loon into a nice bird you would have to begin with the egg, and not a Loon egg, either. Loons do good by keeping people at home nights.

[1] The Loon is not related to the Laughing Jackass or Australian Kingfisher. Mother Nature just happens to have made the same mistake in two birds.

[2] Others regard it as a love call, but I have never seen it do a Loon any good in that way. There always seems to be only one Loon around—a very good reason, however, for sounding a love call.

[3] English ornithologists appear to think that the Loon is the Great Crested Grebe (*Podicipes cristatus*). It is no such thing. The Loon is the Great Northern Diver (*Gavia immer*) or the Common Loon or Dippy the Loon. You can hardly blame the ornithologists for getting confused about such a bird.

THE WATER OUZEL

THE Water Ouzel or Dipper was designed for dry land but he wanted to be a water bird and so that is what he is. Hooray for the Water Ouzel! His feet are not even webbed [1] but he dives [2] into swift mountain streams and walks [3] around on the bottom eating animalculæ, crustaceans and fish eggs. [4] He has an awful time keeping down because he is built like a cork and tends to bob to the surface. Water Ouzels nest behind waterfalls and the young hardly know what to do. Water Ouzels are said to be the most moral [5] of all birds. They are strictly monogamous and some are not even that. [6] During March and April

Water Ouzels pursue each other upstream and down and go *bzeet bzeet.* The South American Water Ouzel is known as Schultz's Dipper. The Irish Ouzel (*Cinclus hibernicus*) migrates to New York. The Hairy Ainu believe that whoever eats the heart of the Water Ouzel will be able to argue down all his opponents.[7] This does not work out because some people cannot be argued down no matter what you eat.

[1] As most of my readers know, it is not necessary to have webbed feet in order to swim. Many swimmers, however, have lobate toes or incipient webs.

[2] The females wade into the water until it is over their heads and then keep right on going. Once thoroughly submerged, they hate to come out.

[3] Some observers state that the bird scrambles, scuffles or tumbles about and others say that he does none of these things. It may be that when an ornithologist says that the Water Ouzel walks under water he only means that he has seen a Water Ouzel or some other bird sitting on a stone in the general vicinity of some body of water.

[4] It has been denied that the Water Ouzel eats the spawn of Trout. I have found that it saves wear and tear to believe all such charges and then make excuses for the accused animal, or not, as the case may be.

[5] To prove this ornithologists make the point that the Water Ouzel continues to sing after the honeymoon, thus indicating that he cares for plenty of things besides passion. This habit may just as well indicate an essentially trivial attitude towards life, hardened cynicism, or even downright immorality—under the water, perhaps.

[6] An Ouzel of my acquaintance appeared to be quite without any thought of sex, interested only in small crustaceans and botany. It turned out later that he was a very old Ouzel and far from well. He had all he could do to fly.

[7] Compare homeopathic magic among the Bahima of Uganda, the Bukaua of New Guinea, the Wotjobaluks of Southeastern Australia and Shrove Tuesday customs in Esthonia.

THE FLAMINGO

FLAMINGOES live in wild and inaccessible spots where we don't have to look at them. They have necks like a Giraffe and legs like a Swede [1] and they honk like a Goose.[2] They fly all stretched out as though they were doing it on a bet. They are pinkish or reddish. Flamingoes are extremely shy but not with each other. They have movable maxillæ and horny lamillæ and they all live together in low mud flats. They post sentinels so that we cannot see what they do. The Chilean Flamingo has no hallux but his tarsus is twelve and a half inches long.[3] Young Flamingoes have regular features but they gradually grow funnier. The starving natives of the Bahamas frequently kill and eat Flamingoes although it is against the law. We must educate these persons to starve and like it. The Emperor Heliogabalus ordered the tongues of fifteen hundred Flamingoes to be served in a single dish. This is said to prove that fish are good for the brain.[4] Flamingoes can be trained but after you have spent years training one all you have is a trained Flamingo.[5]

[1] Some say this is acromegaly, caused by an abnormal discharge of tethelin from the anterior lobe of the pituitary gland or hypophysis, which is attached to the brain by means of the infundibulum. It is more likely that it just runs in the family.

[2] The Ancient Persians called this bird the Red Goose, which is probably about what it is. The Persians were extraordinarily level-headed. You couldn't stampede them with a mere fancy name for a Goose.

[3] I omit further anatomical details. I am not writing a book for people who would be likely to confuse a Flamingo with some other animal. No amount of particulars would help such people.

[4] He also ate the brains of Flamingoes, Ostriches, Parrots, Pheasants and Thrushes but nothing came of it. Perhaps we have here the origin of the term *bird-brain*.

[5] Flamingoes often live for years in captivity, but there are ways of preventing this.

FAREWELL TO BIRDS

*

THE PARROT

THE PENGUIN

THE WOODPECKER

THE DOTTEREL

THE SPARROW

THE HUMMINGBIRD

THE PARROT

T HE Parrot doesn't know what he's talking about but we do. Sometimes he says things that fit in, like anybody else. His language is very broadening if you understand Portuguese. The Parrot's tendency to talk varies inversely as the square of his gray matter. Or rather it would if he had any gray matter.[1] The Parrot mates for life. Parrots are not very passionate. They have truncated mandibles. In the old square-rigger days the Parrot was used as an engagement ring. During a week ashore a sailor would frequently employ as many as forty-nine Parrots in this way in New Bedford alone. Those were called the good old days. The sagacity of the Parrot is well known. He can be taught to imitate a Dog fight, spill the ink, step in the dessert, smash porcelain vases, laugh like a Hyena and say the same thing over and over for hours at a time. He is highly esteemed for his habit of biting out small portions of the human face. Parrots are often improved by rapping them smartly on the merrythought or furcula with a sledge hammer. Parrots reckon time by walnuts, one walnut equalling an hour and a half. They are also fond of papaws, hawthorn berries, peach stones, capsicum and the legs of Hepplewhite chairs.[2] Parrots live two hundred years and finally become heirlooms. You can tell people who have inherited several Parrots.[3]

[1] Aristotle found Parrots more talkative when drunk. They haven't changed much.

[2] The curvilinear contours of Hepplewhite and Chippendale appear to attract Parrots more than the somewhat severer lines of Sheraton. Parrots are even happier with the much more edible Regency and Louis XV pieces.

[3] A Parrot belonging to Dennis O'Kelly, sometimes called Colonel O'Kelly or Count O'Kelly, could sing the 104th Psalm, "The Banks of the Dee" and "God Save the King" with the utmost precision, which was more than Count O'Kelly could do. Count O'Kelly died in 1787, the Parrot surviving until 1802.

PENGUINS are dignified. For all we know they may have a reason. To catch a Penguin off his dignity might take years and would hardly be worth the trouble. In standing the Penguin rests his entire weight on the metatarsus, causing topheaviness and certain nervous disorders. He flies in the water and barks. Penguins are very industrious. They carry sticks and stalks of grass for considerable distances and drop them into the ocean. The males steal stones from other Penguins and present them to the females, to Antarctic explorers and to any other object of interest. The average Penguin has the mind of an eight-year-old child but he gets his picture in the Sunday papers. Parental love exists among Penguins to an unusual degree. The male and female Penguins often come to blows over the privilege of hatching the eggs and caring for the young. They love their offspring so much that many young Penguins crawl away during the night and fall through cracks in the ice.[1] Then it starts all over again. Male Penguins are unfaithful up to an advanced age, a phenomenon sometimes attributed to the sea air. Penguins are well-meaning birds with little or no notion of what is going on. Only the expert can tell a live Penguin from a stuffed one. It is probable that most Penguins are stuffed. Some people nearly die laughing at Penguins.

[1] For this sketch of parental affection among Penguins, and for other bits of information too numerous to mention, I am indebted to Isabel Paterson, whose views on Antarctica are uniformly sound and unfailingly brilliant; but then, which of her views on other regions of the globe may one not describe in exactly the same terms? Perhaps this is the place to state that Mrs. Paterson by no means shares all the author's opinions on bird life. In a recent communication she says that she knows what I mean, and sympathizes profoundly, but that still, at the same time, she can see the birds' side of it, too.

THE WOODPECKER

THE Woodpecker has survived because he has a powerful pygostyle and a long protrusible tongue and a spring in his neck. If he had not survived we could all get some sleep. With his wedgelike bill he bores for insects under the bark of trees, tin roofs and steel girders.[1] He thus protects our forest trees if he has to kill them to do it. The Woodpecker pounds acorns into the sides of trees and then forgets about them but most of his hammering is done for love.[2] For the same reason Woodpeckers go *chink chink, plick plick, ker-ruck* and *prrp prrp*. The Scaly-cheeked Plumbeous Woodpecker of Transcaspia goes *tjupk tjupk tjupk*. Love is like that in Transcaspia. The Woodpecker's home life is ideal. The male hovers nearby and makes contented sounds while the female is chopping trees for a nest, but look who he is. The Red-headed Woodpecker beats his wife.[3] The Downy Woodpecker is rather cute. He hangs around feeding shelves and suet containers. He whinnies. The Woodpecker lives for seventy years, so that if you are very young you have a chance to outlast him.[4]

[1] In a way it seems awful that an insect cannot feel safe even under the bark of a tree. Mother Nature, however, has equipped the Woodpecker to get in there and get him, and at the same time has equipped the insect to stay there and be eaten.

[2] In a recent number of *Nature* (May, 1880) on the habits of the Lesser Spotted Woodpecker the Duke of Argyll very properly observes that the tapping of this animal appears to take the place of the vernal song. He suggests that it is intended as a serenade to the Lesser Spotted Woodpecker's wife, sitting at home on the eggs. Let us hope so.

[3] Not a little discussion has been aroused by the fact that in Europe some of the Woodpeckers migrate East and West instead of North and South, as is customary with birds. This need cause no alarm. In Europe it is quite the natural thing to do. Cuckoos have been migrating East and West in Europe for centuries.

[4] The natives of Hudson's Bay call the Golden-winged Woodpecker the *Ou-thee-quan-nor-ow* for reasons best known to themselves.

THE DOTTEREL

DOTTERELS have no sense whatever. They know in a vague sort of way that something happened in 1492 because something happens *every* year but the details are all a blur. The Dotterel lets himself get caught by all kinds of people because he is too trusting. He walks right up to them in the belief that they want to take him on a visit to the Bok Bird Sanctuary. As a result of this habit the Dotterel will soon be extinct and nobody will care much excepting the members of the Save the Dotterel Movement.[1] Dotterels swallow grit and have pervious nostrils and something is wrong with their pineal glands. The Dotterel makes wigwag motions with his wings and legs but nobody knows what he means. Whatever it is, it is wrong.[2] Dotterels inhabit the mountainous regions of Transylvania and Bohemia. They winter in Palestine and Egypt. Sometimes they start for Palestine and wind up in Senegambia or the Moluccas or Mozambique or Tierra del Fuego. The female Dotterel is larger and stronger than the male.[3] She takes entire charge of the courtship and subsequent events. The male Dotterel hatches the eggs, brings up the young and does the housework and is therefore known as the Lesser Sap.[4] Sometimes he utters a low plaintive whistle.[5]

[1] My readers may remember what happened to the Great Bustard for being just the opposite, too wary. I think it will be agreed that the moral is not a very cheering one. It seems you can't beat the game.

[2] It was formerly thought that he was imitating the actions of the fowler, but he hasn't that much brains. It is not improbable that these gestures have a sexual significance. Or he may be throwing something into gear or out of gear.

[3] The Dotterel is strictly monogamous. There ought to be a lesson in that somewhere.

[4] The Dotterel weighs only four ounces. It has long been a scientific riddle how so much utter wrong-headedness can manage to exist in so small a space. Still, there's the Least Gnatcatcher.

[5] Other foolish birds include the Semipalmated Plover, the Marbled Godwit, the Carolina Mosshead, the Tasmanian Googlenose and the Fool Hen or Franklin Grouse of the Rockies.

THE SPARROW

TO the seeing eye life is mostly Sparrows. The average Sparrow is something of a bore and the trouble is that all Sparrows are average. The Sparrow has been called the bird in the street because he sits on telephone wires. The early morning anthem of the Song Sparrow tells us that it is time to get up and close the windows and go back to bed. The English Sparrow drives away our native songbirds. He is regarded as a pest by those who like our native songbirds. The Social or Chipping Sparrow chases insects on the wing and seldom catches them. He goes *chippy chippy chippy*. The White-throated Sparrow goes *Old Sam Peabody Peabody Peabody*.[1] Other Sparrows go *tweet tweet, tsip tsip* and *chee chee*. The Ipswich Sparrow is found in Ipswich. The ability to distinguish the different kinds of Sparrows is believed to be an inherited character.[2] The Sparrow is very keen about you know what. To the male and even in greater degree to the female love is all. For other important things here below, if there are any, he doesn't give a single *tweet*.[3] When a Sparrow comes to die, at least he can say that he has lived.[4] There is nothing wrong with his corpus striatum. Sparrows all roost together in large trees because they believe it helps their mental development.

[1] To others this call sounds more like *Oh hear me Theresa Theresa Theresa*, or *clink clink*. Persons who decide such matters are said to be fey or Ph.D.'s. Among the Trobriand Islanders their food is treated with a certain highly poisonous herb.

[2] Anyway, it seems to run in certain old New England families, the members of which are generally natural born Sparrow-distinguishers.

[3] Or it may be some other bird that goes *tweet* all the time. The author of this volume does not pretend to be a *tweet* expert. He may be thinking of the Green-tailed Towhee.

[4] They must have their little tragedies, though. Imagine yourself a Sparrow madly in love with another Sparrow, who gets lost. All about you are millions of other Sparrows all looking exactly like your predestined mate. Still, one can see how that might work out, so why worry?

THE Hummingbird flits from flower to flower like some exquisite jewel, filling his little gizzard with Ants, Snout Beetles, Thrips, Spiders and Plant-lice.[1] He has long served as the symbol of innocence and a splendid example to American youth. Of the Committee of Nineteen appointed to investigate the private life of this feathered sprite, eight fainted dead away and eleven went native.[2] The details would have to be printed in a book for men only.[3] Hummingbirds work on Sunday, carry pollen between male and female flowers and indulge in mixed bathing. They have very deep carinæ and their faces lack expression. The male is colored much more gorgeously than the female so that he can be shot and made into feather embroidery.[4] Hummingbirds can fly backwards and sideways. They are ferocious fighters, weighing in at about twenty-five grains.[5] The Ruby-throated Hummingbird is a Don Juan type. He has a slight squeak which is said to mean *fiddle-de-dee*. The Hermit Hummingbird of Venezuela has a curved beak, a cuneate tail and buff underparts. Helena's Hummingbird of Costa Rica is about two inches long. Allowing for the bill and the tail, this leaves practically nothing to write about.[6]

[1] The popular notion that this animal lives entirely upon honey-dew is erroneous. He can hardly help getting a certain amount of nectar with his insects. Honey-dew, indeed!

[2] Much still remains to be learned about his sex life because the Hummingbird is quicker than the eye.

[3] Hummingbirds are always warmer than we are because the necessity of continual oxidation or combustion of carbohydrate material, that is to say, the ratio of the katabolism to the— anyway, their temperature runs from 100° to 113° Fahrenheit.

[4] Among the Ancient Mexicans the Hummingbird was known as the Hoitzitziltototl. Wouldn't he have been?

[5] It has frequently been remarked that the smaller Hummingbirds are about the size of a large Bee. Eliza Cook caught this idea very neatly in her line, "Hummingbirds scarcely are larger than bees." Mrs. Hemans also left us some fairly perishable lines on the bird.

[6] Professor R. S. Lull states: "In relation to bodily weight, man's brain exceeds that of any other creature except some excessively small vertebrates such as the Humming Birds and smaller Mice." You can take that any way you like.

WILD BEASTS I HAVE MET

*

A T the last minute I have decided to omit my thrilling adventures with Grizzlies out West. I am afraid that entirely too much romance, sentiment —imagination, you might even say—would inevitably creep into the story. Still, there was that time in Wyoming— No, it won't do.

Besides, who cares if they did call me Grizzly Will? In the good old days—(Note to printer: If I say anything more about the good old days, just quietly cut it out. Those *were* the days, though, weren't they?)

But no fooling, I should like to clear up some rumors. I have heard it said that I have practically never seen a wild beast in my life, that I am always confusing the Duck-billed Platypus with the Ai or Three-toed Sloth and that my knowledge of the chase has been confined exclusively to swatting Flies. Most of this is simply not true. I have seen lots of animals.

Take the Blue or Brindled Gnu. Didn't I dash to

Madison Square Garden to investigate him before I set pen to paper? In the first place, he wasn't blue, as I might have known; that was too much to hope for, and I was a fool to expect it. He was not a very nice Gnu, either. He didn't like me. I'm rather psychic about those things, especially when an animal is trying to burst from his cage on purpose to murder me. I wouldn't put anything past that Gnu.

I gained from this ghastly visit little more than the conviction that Blue or Brindled Gnus may be all right in their place. It's a mistake to meet them.

My conscience is clear about Beavers, at any rate. The hours I've sat at my desk and thought about Beavers, you wouldn't believe. For sheer unadulterated struggle and the total elapsed time it took me to write up the Beaver I defy you to name another author and any two animals. The experience has left its mark. "You must think like a Beaver" is the first rule in this line of endeavor. That's easy enough. The trouble comes in unbeavering oneself.

What is more, I almost saw a Beaver, and a cruel hot day it was to go traipsing to Bronx Park. I saw the Beaver pond and some lovely Bears—in fact, that's where I encountered the Grizzly; but no Beaver, and very few signs of a Beaver. It seems that the Beavers come out after dark and the Zoo closes at seven, at least it did that day. Whether the keepers would have let me stay all night so that I could say I'd seen a Beaver, I don't know. Maybe they would.

I can assure you that Beaver biographers are not the happy, carefree bunch some people fancy them.

They have to take their knocks. Only recently an anonymous gentleman has informed the press that everything ever written about Beavers is what he is pleased to call a pack of falsehoods; largely, he holds, because authors are not sufficiently familiar with the beast.

This raises a question. It may be desirable that anyone who writes about Beavers should actually have seen one or more Beavers in operation. I say it may. I'm not at all sure. Conditions are changing. Few of us have either the time or the opportunity to move to Beaver-infested regions and stand around for months on the off chance of watching a Beaver gnaw a piece of wood. For my part, I'm not enthusiastic about it. I'm afraid Beavers would depress me horribly.

If that anonymous gentleman has been privileged to see a Beaver, let him offer up silent thanks instead of saying nasty things about those of us to whom Life has not been so bountiful. He may know all about Beavers, but he displays a touching ignorance of literature. For him the classic tradition in such matters appears to have rumbled down the centuries in vain. How does he think animal books are written, anyway? By whom? And why?

I have come across a paragraph which speaks volumes on this point. It was a Mr. Cumberland who observed of Oliver Goldsmith and his invaluable, if now somewhat antiquated work, "A History of the Earth and Animated Nature":

"Distress drove Goldsmith upon undertakings

neither congenial with his studies nor worthy of his talents. I remember him when, in his chambers in the Temple, he showed me the beginning of his 'Animated Nature;' it was with a sigh, such as genius draws when hard necessity diverts it from its bent to drudge for bread, and talk of birds, and beasts, and creeping things, which Pidock's showman would have done as well. Poor fellow, he hardly knows an Ass from a Mule, nor a Turkey from a Goose, but when he sees it on the table."

But there were those who didn't mind all that about our Noll. They rallied round. Dr. Johnson gave him some stern and rockbound advice, particularly as to the close relation existing between cause and effect, in a free-for-all arising from the alleged custom among the natives of Otaheite of eating Dogs. On another occasion the Panjandrum silenced the buzzing Boswell with this little piece of his mind: "Sir, he has the art of compiling, and of saying everything he has to say in a pleasing manner. He is now writing a Natural History, and will make it as entertaining as a Persian tale."

In the long run what did it matter whether Goldsmith knew the Yak? He knew Dr. Johnson!

The reviews were fair. Says Washington Irving— no mean critic—of Goldsmith's volume: "Though much of it was borrowed from Buffon, and but little of it written from his own observation; though it was by no means profound, and was chargeable with many errors, yet—"

Do you, fellow book reviewers, get the full effect, the poignant, haunting beauty, of that "yet"? I have no intention of trying to sway your judgment about any book—no special book, just any book; but never forget, Best Beloved, in the name of all that is human, that we have in our language that wonderful word, "yet."

Space lacks in which to deal with the Aristotelean tradition as it so richly deserves, a tradition to which it is my earnest hope that I have done as little violence as possible, in spots. Suffice it that Aristotle seems always to have had in mind an Ideal Wombat. This animal, through changing winds of doctrine, Nominalism and Realism, gradually developed into an Absolute, and finally, over a long period of years and by a slow process of attrition, became the *Ding an Sich* or Square-mouthed Rhinoceros.

I release my pieces, then, with all their faults upon them, from no wish to impose upon the credulous, but in the ordinary give and take of the business. My horror of disseminating untruth in its cruder forms is as great as yours, but what can one do?

Could I help spilling my indexed notes in a high wind and getting them hopelessly mixed? Some of those notes were awful examples of what you must on no account believe. Others were taken straight from the animal. Now who knows which from which? Where you catch me in flagrant instances, I should like to point out that there isn't much to be said in favor of facts. I have always maintained, and I still maintain, that vital statistics about animals are largely states of mind.

For other lies I am more to blame. Having polished off one animal, I am afraid I was not always strong enough to resist the temptation of putting the left-overs into the next. On the other hand, I may boast of some trifling constructive work. When I felt that the expert testimony conflicted too wildly with what I had always heard, I have managed to strike a balance which should be satisfactory.

My free and easy classifications may disturb a few. Why did I place the birds between the primates and the lesser mammals? Why did I leave the Bats until the last, when they belong to the Chiroptera, near the top? I need but mention the name of the Great Buffon, who observed little or no method unless he got up feeling exactly like it.

If M. de Buffon wished to begin the day with the Horse and leave the Zebra for Chapter XVII, several volumes later, between the Tapir and the Hippopotamus, he did so, and that was all there was to it. If, at any time or place, he desired to interpolate a sizable essay upon the Bezoar Stone or other pressing problem, you could read it and like it. M. de Buffon was a man who soared far above the trammels of mere system. So was King Solomon. So, in his small way, is a certain humble follower.

Let's have no talk of precedents, then. I have plenty of precedents. Where I have departed from them I really feel that I have arranged the animals more in accordance with the needs of today. Besides, what else matters if you have your health?

MAMMALS YOU OUGHT TO KNOW

or

WHY BE A RHINOCEROS?

*

THE LION
THE TIGER
THE ELEPHANT
THE RHINOCEROS
THE HIPPOPOTAMUS
THE GIRAFFE

THE LION

THE Lion is called the King of Beasts because that is the main thing about him. He inhabits the Torrid Zone and is fond of Zebras and Hottentots. Lions once lived in Egypt, where they symbolized the annual inundation of the Nile or Ptah. The natives would sing Egyptian songs to them and they gradually left the country. Ptolemy VI arranged a parade of several thousand Lions and several hundred virgins.

The Lion has tactile facial vibrissæ or whiskers provided with large nerve-bulbs about the size of a pea. If you examine these closely for several moments your time hasn't come yet.[1] The Lion is a generous foe because he kills with one blow of his paw and does not bear a grudge. He will not hurt you unless he is hungry or wounded or frightened or annoyed or vicious.[2] The Lion is a Cat or Feline but he seems more like a Dog. When he lashes his sides with his tail strangers often rush up and pet him. They do this only once.[3] The Lion is sometimes described as cowardly and mean because he does not care to be shot. Some people lose all respect for the Lion unless he devours them instantly. There is no pleasing some people. The Lion should be let alone. He was there first.[4]

[1] Aristotle maintains that the neck of the Lion is composed of a single bone. Aristotle knew nothing at all about Lions, a circumstance which did not prevent him from writing a good deal on the subject.

[2] The problem of the Lion's temperament is somewhat difficult. A Lion once shook Dr. Livingstone severely. On the other hand, we have Androcles, Daniel and Corey Ford. Pliny remarks of the Lion that "his usual state is that of rage"; yet Nero, the Lion exhibited with Wombwell's Travelling Menagerie, was exceedingly docile and affectionate.

[3] The desire to romp with Lions when they are seen bounding across their native heath appears to be widespread among tourists. It is difficult to take bounding animals seriously, but if one doesn't, they are likely to have the last laugh.

[4] In South Africa, which is colonized by the Boers, or Dutch, a Lion hunt is largely a matter of *spoors, kloofs, kraals* and the like. In his interesting account of a Cape Lion hunt, Mr. Pringle tells how he had the misfortune to employ a party of Bastuards, or Mulatto Hottentots, who tracked the beasts to a large *bosch*, or bush, but at the first sign of danger turned and fled, with the utmost show of pusillanimity. Mr. Pringle seems to have been blissfully unaware of the nature of Bastuards.

THE TIGER

TIGERS are very beautiful but when they are bad they are horrid. They are very voluptuous because they do not know any better. They commit rapine and pillage and have two or more cubs at a time. Tigers live in Asia in *nullahs* and *sholos*. They seldom climb trees but don't count on that. There is no use saying "Boo!" to a Tiger. It only makes him worse. The Siberian Tiger is found near Blagovyeshchensk and the Sea of Okhotsk but not in Omsk.[1] The Man-eating Tiger is old and decrepit. He has lost his strength and vigor and we should feel sorry for him. Young normal Tigers do not eat people. If eaten by a Tiger you may rest assured that he was abnormal. Once in a while a normal Tiger will eat somebody but he doesn't mean anything by it.[2] Tiger cubs play with old tires and go *Pff-ffst!* Persons who raise Tiger cubs in their homes are sometimes known as missing persons. The Leopard or Pard is bearded.[3] The Snow Leopard or Ounce has greenish eyes. Among the Llanero Indians of South America the youth who kills seven Jaguars becomes a *guapo*, with the privilege of choosing the fattest maiden of the tribe as his companion. Sometimes there are so many new *guapos* that the thinner girls get a chance.[4]

[1] Miss Elsie McCormick, an excellent judge of such things, regards the Siberian Tiger as the most ferocious of the *Felidæ*. She rightly considers the Royal Bengal Tiger a mere upstart, since the Ancient Hindus know nothing about him. There is no word for Tiger in Sanskrit.

[2] There is always the danger that a perfectly normal Tiger will turn abnormal while in your immediate neighborhood. Since Tigers prefer dark persons, it is advisable, when sleeping in Asia, always to be accompanied by several native friends.

[3] So, for that matter, are the other Felines. A keen observer has noted that all owners of whiskers, or facial vibrissæ, appear to have uncanny skill at distinguishing objects during their nocturnal wanderings and generally getting about in the dark.

[4] A gentleman going abroad presented his pet Tiger to the Tower of London, where the growing beast came to be looked upon as insatiably cruel and quite incorrigible. Returning to England after three years, the former owner, to the great consternation of the keeper, boldly entered the Tiger's cage, and that was the last of *him*.

THE Elephant is very intelligent because he does whatever you tell him to do. He carries teakwood logs in his mouth and reaches for peanuts and never forgets.[1] Without his trunk the Elephant would be in a pretty fix. That is why he has it. Wild Elephants crush everybody who gets in their way. Tame Elephants crush only certain people. The Elephant has a kind face but his brain is relatively small and old-

(123)

fashioned.[2] His head is filled with large spaces which in turn are filled with air. As he goes through life and gains experience he keeps adding more air. After bathing he throws dust on his back. The Elephant has been called the most respectable of all creatures excepting us. When so large an animal is respectable he is very much so indeed. The opposite also holds true.[3] At birth an Elephant is only three feet high and weighs but three hundred pounds. Grown Elephants vary in size. Jumbo was twelve feet six inches high when Mr. Barnum measured him and ten feet nine at other times. The Indian or Circus Elephant is called a Ponderous Performing Pachyderm.[4] He has whitewashed toes. The African or Corrugated Elephant is fidgety. The Rogue Elephant has original ideas and may be shot at sight.

[1] Having swallowed a quantity of burning hot gingerbread nuts presented to him by a conceited youth named John Doe, an Elephant bided his time and five years later took what he thought to be a sufficient revenge. But for once the joke was on the Elephant, whose victim proved to be, not John Doe, but his cousin, Richard Roe, who much resembled him.

[2] Actually, the brain of an Elephant is twice as large as that of a Man. This does not mean, however, that all Elephants are twice as smart as all Men, a condition obtaining only among exceptional Elephants.

[3] Elephants are inordinately fond of arrack. The Mandrill prefers porter and gin, while Baboons and Hedgehogs demand beer. Other intemperate vertebrates include the Sooty Mangabey, the Raccoon and the Horse. Sir Stamford Raffles owned a Malayan Sun Bear who would drink only champagne. Very few animals know when they have had enough.

[4] In Asia the Elephant carries a *mahout* seated upon a *gadella* and armed with a *hawkuss* or *haunkus* or *gujbag*; and, occasionally, a *maharajah* in a *howdah*. *Goondahs* or adult males are often captured with the help of *koomkies* or trained females. The technique of the *koomkies* can hardly be described in a work of this nature.

THE RHINOCEROS

THE Rhinoceros is something fierce. His hide is two inches thick. He cannot take a hint or be insulted or have his feelings hurt. His expression lacks all charm and his profile is utterly hopeless. Rhinoceroses are dull of sight but their hearing is keen and their scent is powerful. They do not know their own strength. Some Rhinos will charge when provoked and others will gallop away and it is a good thing to know which is which. You cannot argue with them because they do not get the finer shades.[1] Rhinos do not mate for life but they manage. They are very happy at first.[2] When angry they snort and tear up bushes and plunge about in dense thickets. Then they feel better.[3] The skin of the One-horned Indian or Armor-plated Rhinoceros is folded at the shoulders and thighs and other strategic points. It is always like that.[4] The Two-horned Black Rhinoceros eats thistles

(125)

and thorns and is very irritable. The White or Square-mouthed Rhinoceros of Zululand is battleship gray or light reddish-brown. He eats only grass and is becoming extinct. The Rhinoceros is brought from foreign lands and kept at the Zoo with his name in large letters so that people can say, "Oh, see the Hippo-potamus!"

[1] In hunting any savage beast, one should first ascertain the animal's plans and then act accordingly. If a Rhino has decided to charge, jump aside at the proper instant, and his impetus will carry him past you. After several charges, however, his impetus will become much less, and there you are.

[2] It has been well said that you never really know a Rhinoceros until you live with one.

[3] The Rhinoceros is generally regarded as quite untameable. It is probable that any animal whatever can be tamed if one is willing to go to the time and trouble. Unfortunately, one is likely to lose interest in that particular animal before one can prove it. Or one may wish to tame some entirely different animal.

[4] The Rhinoceros is set in his way. He walks in his own tracks day after day, starting for his favorite water hole at exactly 4 P.M. The philosopher Kant, inventor of the *Ding an Sich*, always started his *Spatziergang* just half an hour earlier, at 3:30 P.M.

THE HIPPOPOTAMUS

T HE Hippopotamus is fat and good-natured. He
 has seven wives or a total of twenty-one tons.
His femur is flat. The Hippopotamus looks monogamous. He looks as if he would have to be.[1] How he
can appeal to seven other Hippopotamuses is his own
secret.[2] He keeps most of his face under water. Hippopotamuses cannot bear to be alone for obvious reasons.
They prefer to live in herds even though this involves

being with other Hippopotamuses. They pass the time floating around and yawning and blowing bubbles in the Nile and the Zambesi and the Limpopo. They think that nothing else matters. They have primitive minds because they live in such awful places. They have no clavicles and they care less.[3] Hippos like fun. They love to submerge and reappear in unexpected spots. On the way up they will bite a chunk out of your catamaran or canoe. The Pigmy Hippopotamus inhabits Liberia and the Bronx. The Hippopotamus is the largest living non-ruminating even-toed ungulate mammal and what does it get him? His hide is made into *jamboks* or *sjamboks* by the Ajumba. This animal reminded the Ancient Greeks of a Horse, so they called him the River Horse. What a Horse reminded them of is unknown.[4]

[1] I am aware that the Encyclopædia Hippopotamus is monogamous. In this article I have relied partly upon intuition and partly upon Nigerian folklore, which seldom goes wrong on such matters—the Nigerians make it a life work.

[2] How he can appeal even to one appears scarcely less extraordinary. Unprepossessing as he may be, the Hippo has a friendly look, and that atones for a great deal. Another point in his favor is that the Rhinoceros is even homelier.

[3] But he has a huckle-bone or astragalus and your guess is as good as mine.

[4] The Reverend M. G. Watkins states that Behemoth of the Book of Job was not the Hippopotamus, after all, but the Mammoth, since the letters *b* and *m* are interchangeable in Arabic. Here we have a beautiful demonstration of Grimm's Law, discovered by Isabel Paterson in 1920.

THE GIRAFFE

THE Giraffe or Camelopard is rather fantastic but who isn't? Giraffes are so tall because their ancestors ate the top branches of trees. The shorter Giraffes could not reach the top branches and died off. Why the shorter Giraffes did not eat the tops of shorter trees seems very strange. Perhaps it never occurred to them.[1] When standing beside a mimosa the Giraffe is indistinguishable from the tree except that he has four legs and a head and a tail. Some hunters will stalk a mimosa tree for days without getting results. Others take to stalking apple trees. The Giraffe is vague and fitful. He never knows what he may do next.[2] The herd is governed by an experienced male who is governed by several experienced females. The males spend the months of April and May in kicking each other in the shins. The young are born in June of the following year.[3] The Northern or Reticulated Giraffe is almost completely reticulated. The Southern or Blotchy Giraffe has large liquid brown eyes and they don't mean a thing.[4] Among the N'jemps of Legumukum Giraffes are regarded as sacred because they are worth so much money. A first class guaranteed Giraffe will cost you about fifteen thousand dollars. What this country needs is a good medium-priced Giraffe.[5]

[1] The Giraffe's neck invariably strikes a certain type of mind as a subject for dubious jests about tonsilitis and the like. Theoretically, at least, it should be possible to discuss this feature of the Giraffe without recourse to loud and vacant laughter. Nevertheless there seems little excuse for so much neck in any one animal.

[2] Giraffes worry a good deal about the Machine Age. They simply do not understand people who say, "Isn't it wonderful—all these new inventions?" To a Giraffe any invention of whatever nature is rank poison. He may decide to become extinct.

[3] Curiously, most animals are born in the spring, although it is often stated that animals cannot count. If that is so, then how do the parents figure out—I mean to say, why do they always—anyway, it turns out all right.

[4] Of the Giraffe's rather sentimental facial expression, an authority remarks, "He seems to reflect, to think, to deliberate." Well, you could say that of almost anybody!

[5] As a pet, the Giraffe can be overdone. They are somewhat conspicuous, and the cheaper grades have a tendency to attract moths. They will eat forage biscuits, cereals, mulberry leaves, artificial flowers and paint. The worst of it is, people keep shouting at you, "Where did you get that Giraffe?"

FAIR TO MEDIUM MAMMALS

*

THE POLAR BEAR
THE BEAVER
THE GNU
THE WHALE
THE ZEBRA

THE POLAR BEAR

THE Polar Bear has a very low freezing point. When others are all over chilblains he's complaining of the heat. His favorite seat is a cake of ice and he never has chilblains but he has crazy spells. Polar Bears live mostly upon Seals. It is a good thing to keep out of the Arctic if you look like a Seal. Polar Bears mature much later than animals near the Equator. Some Polar Bears live so far North that they never mature. The best ones are made into rugs for people to trip over. Some Polar Bears do not wish to be rugs. They never amount to much. The Kodiak Bear or Great Huge Bear inhabits Kodiak Island. The fur of the Brown or Middle-sized Bear is used for busbies by the British and Kamchatkans. The Kamchatkans wear thin Bearskin masks to protect their faces from the sun. Why the Kamchatkans should wish

to protect their faces is unknown.[1] Bears will not eat
Kamchatkans.[2] Grizzly Bears eat blueberries.[3] The
Malayan Sun Bear or Little Small Wee Bear eats apri-
cots, honey, porridge, mangosteens and chocolate
almond bars. Bears are never bored in the Zoo because they see such funny sights.[4]

[1] Kamchatkans are really at their best when wearing these
facial coverings. In addition to Bears, Kamchatkans have fogs,
famines, volcanoes, epidemics of Arctic hysteria, whortleber-
ries and radios.

[2] The Brown Bear is able to sense the presence of a Kamchatkan even when he (the Kamchatkan) is well to leeward.

[3] I do not believe that Bears hibernate nearly so much as
they are said to do. Nowadays any animal observed in a torpid,
lethargic or semi-comatose condition is immediately accused of
hibernating, when ten to one he isn't. Semi-comatose states are
perfectly normal with some species at all times.

[4] I have never cared for the prophet Elisha since that epi-
sode of the two She Bears who chastised the forty and two
children who mocked him. "Go up, thou baldhead" is not a
very nice thing to say to a prophet, but Elisha needn't have
cursed them in the name of the Lord—and that's what brought
the She Bears out of the wood. Mr. Frank Finn, B.A. (Oxon),
F.Z.S., thinks that the attack of these Bears may have taken
the form of scalping. "Thus," he remarks, "there would be a
curious appropriateness in the irreverent youngsters being
made prematurely bald." I hardly know what to think of
Mr. Finn.

THE BEAVER

THE Beaver is very industrious but he is still a
Beaver. His brain is quite smooth. The Beaver
works hard all his life and finally becomes a deceased
Beaver.[1] Beavers possess marked engineering talents
but they are weak in arithmetic. They build dams
which flood the surrounding country, drown the forests, ruin the crops and impede navigation. Beavers

are glowing examples.[2] After completing a dam they remain nearby until they are trapped by the Hudson's Bay Company. The Beaver is called *O-bo-ye-wa* or *Gi-chi-ah-mik* by the natives of Michigan, who are called *Ojibways* or *Chippeways*.[3] Beavers keep people awake nights by flapping their tails on the water. In winter they stay in their houses or lodges eating wood and having mange.[4] During the month of February Beavers act very strangely. The tympanic bulla is globular and larger than in Man. Young Beavers are born with their eyes open. At the age of one year they know everything.[5]

[1] To give the Beaver his due, he does things because he has to do them, not because he believes that hard work *per se* will somehow make him a better Beaver—the Beaver may be dumb, but he is not that dumb! The Beaver was made to gnaw, and gnaw he does. There you have him in a nutshell.

[2] Beaver authorities or Professors of Beaverism frequently introduce a few pardonable touches of hyperbole into their accounts of this rodent. They think nothing of devoting forty or fifty years to the subject; naturally, anything that isn't a Beaver seems all wrong to them.

[3] Binny, a young male Beaver domesticated by a Mr. Brod-leip, in 1825, was accustomed to build dams in the drawing-room. These structures consisted mostly of sweeping-brushes, warming-pans, rush baskets, books, boots, articles of clothing, and bits of coal, string, hay, cotton and dried turf. Luckily for Binny, Mr. Brodleip encouraged these manifestations.

[4] For a brief and pithy exposition of everything that is not true about Beavers, see "A Natural History of Animals" by John Bigland, author of "A View of the World" and "Letters on Universal History." As so often occurs with authors, Mr. Bigland was better on Universal History than on Beavers.

[5] Pliny the Elder tells us that the Pontic Beaver had a nasty bite (*horrendus morsus*). I do not know whether Pliny the Elder had actually been bitten by a Pontic Beaver or just put that in as a warning to Pliny the Younger.

THE Gnu belongs to the Antelope branch of the Hollow-horned Ruminants. He is the fool of the family. He looks like spare parts of a Buffalo and a Pony and that might mean anything. Gnus [1] get excited about nothing at all. When in this state they rush to and fro, pursue one another in circles, paw the air, kick up their heels and scour madly across the plains. Then they come back as if nothing had happened. [2] They keep this up for fifty or sixty years. [3] The Gnu is extremely curious. He climbs to the tops of Ant-hills looking for objects to be curious about. He will risk his life to find out what is what. This is

(137)

seldom worth finding out but the Gnu doesn't mind. The male Gnu can be distinguished from the female at a distance of half a mile. He is larger and darker. They have one at a time. Gnus eat on the bias and have rinderpest. They associate with Ostriches and Quaggas and other mental defectives. Some people fear that the White-tailed Gnu and the White-bearded Gnu and the Brindled Gnu will soon become extinct. They needn't worry. Such things go on forever.[4]

[1] One notes a growing tendency among the young to speak of the Gnu, especially the White-tailed variety, as the Wildebeest. I don't mind saying that this movement will receive no support from those of us who were brought up on plain, old-fashioned Gnus. Wildebeest, indeed!

[2] Commenting upon the popular belief that the Gnu is insane, W. Lauder Lindsay, M.D., F.R.S.E., F.L.S., Honorary Member of the New Zealand Institute—there are no Gnus in New Zealand!—remarks, "It is contrary to all analogy to suppose that any animal species, as a *species*—in other words, that all the individuals of a species are normally mad, however eccentric their behavior." In discussing this subject Gnu experts often display a sagacity not much inferior to that of the Gnu itself.

[3] For valuable information regarding the habits and customs of retired Gnu-hunters named Colonel Sir Francis Pashley-Drake, of Bludleigh Court, Lesser Bludleigh, Goresby-on-the-Ouse, Bedfordshire, I am indebted to Chapter V in "Mr. Mulliner Speaking" (1930) by Mr. P. G. Wodehouse. It seems likely that the uncontrollable desire to hunt Gnus arises either from a superabundance or a complete lack of Gnus in the infantile environment.

[4] Gnus are used chiefly by a certain class of authors for making atrocious puns, such as "No Gnus is good Gnus" and "Happy Gnu Year!" This will go on forever, too, because you can't teach an old Gnu tricks.

THE WHALE

THE Whale is a mammal because we know so much nowadays. If we did not he would still be a fish. At the age of eighteen months our children are taught to say "The Whale is a mammal." Those who refuse are called problem children. The Whale's pectoral fins contain rudimentary fingers or digits. This proves that he is not a fish.[1] Or does it? [2] He also has several small globular spleens and starboard and larboard flukes. The Whale is captured by hurling toggle-irons, gun-bollard heads, swivels, winches and bowsprits and shouting "Thar she blows!" [3] Sometimes the Whale was last seen going Northwest. Whales are silly once every two years. The young are called Short-heads or Baby Blimps. Many Whale romances begin in Baffin's Bay and end in Procter and Gamble's factory, Staten Island. The Great Blue or Sulphur-bottom Whale is a

Baleen or Whalebone Whale. He is a hundred feet long and cannot see his dorsal fin.[4] The Sperm Whale's head is asymmetrical and one-third of his entire length. It is filled with fatty tissue and spermaceti. The Pigmy Sperm Whale has an incomplete zygoma and is not very popular. Grampuses breathe noisily and are found in Atlantic City.

[1] The Whale's pelvis is likewise vestigial. It does seem as though a mammal, if it should have any one thing—but the cetologists say no.

[2] Mr. John Bigland remarks that the present classification of the Whale as a mammal seems "not sufficiently to coincide with the general ideas entertained on this subject." Just what I've been saying.

[3] The Koryaks of Northeastern Siberia (a form of Kamchatkans) propitiate the soul of the dead Whale by blaming it all on the Russians. Conditions are much the same among the Dyaks and Ostiaks.

[4] Pliny the Elder described a Whale called "Balæna or Whirlpool, which is so long and broad as to take up more in length and breadth than two acres of ground." This brings up again the old question: Are the classics doomed? Our ancestors believed that four years of this sort of information would inevitably produce a President, or at least a Cabinet Member. It didn't seem to work out that way.

THE ZEBRA

Z IS for Zebra. The Zebra is a small striped Horse[1] or Donkey. He lives in Africa. The Zebra is striped all over so that the Lion can see him and eat him. Some people say he is striped so that the Lion can *not* see him. These people believe that the stripes of the Zebra simulate the bars of sunlight falling through the tall jungle grasses and that therefore the Zebra is invisible and that the earth is flat. This is called the ruptive or obliterative school of thought. According to it any object officially classed as invisible becomes so until further notice.[2] Male

Zebras fight duels for love and the winner gets kicked in the nose. Zebras mingle with Ostriches and Gnus because they will mingle with anything. Zebras have withers and cruppers and pasterns and warts on the forelegs.[3] They bark. The Mountain Zebra inhabits mountainous regions and limps on the off side. He is black and white. Burchell's Zebra is beige and brown and looks better in pink. The Quagga is now extinct because he was such an ass.[4] He was fond of plantain. Circus Zebras are beautiful and stupid and stubborn. They can act if you lead them around. Zebras are sticklers for etiquette. At the water-hole the males drink first and then the females and then the others.[5]

[1] Horses were introduced into Egypt by the Hyksos or Shepherd Kings (Cf. *Le Cheval*, Paris, 1886). For the paleontology of the Horse see *How To Be a Hermit*.

[2] Zebra fans tend to become extravagant in their statements about the animal. Miss Florence Brobeck has so often told me about the time she addressed the International Zebra Protective Coloration Society that I'm beginning to believe it myself. Aside from this little foible, Florence is one of the smartest writers, talkers and lookers going. Maybe she really did address the I. Z. P. C. S.

[3] Writers who wish to be funnier about the Zebra than I am will do well to mention Sing Sing, fresh paint, barbers' poles and so on. And you can always get a laugh by asking whether Zebras are black striped with white or white striped with black. If writing for highbrows say that George Moore thought Zebras could not be used in art. As a matter of fact, it's so easy that I could do it myself.

[4] Opinions differ on the number of species of the Ass (*Equus asinus*). A conservative estimate is about 17,000.

[5] Some parts of Africa are almost entirely composed of Zebras and Dutch settlers. The Dutch settlers shoot the Zebras for spoiling the crops. As stated above, Zebras are extremely handsome, and that is more than can be said for the Dutch settlers.

AWFUL MAMMALS

*

THE DUCK-BILLED PLATYPUS
THE SLOTH
THE HYENA
THE BAT
THE AARD-VARK

THE DUCK-BILLED PLATYPUS

THE Duck-billed Platypus or Ornithorhyncus [1] of Australia proves that if you are a mammal and lay eggs there is bound to be talk. Mammals should be viviparous but Duck-billed Platypuses are oviparous and so they have been placed in the lowest grade [2] of the class Mammalia with the Echidna or Spiny Ant-eater.[3] They cannot help it but that is a poor excuse.[4] The Platypus is stranger than fiction. He has webbed feet and T-shaped interclavicles and brown eyes and a spur on the tarsus used during courtship and marriage. He has no corpus callosum and no external ear and very little sense. He is set in his way. He should have become extinct in the Pliocene but he wouldn't. Platypuses build nests of grass and nelumbium leaves in burrows on the banks of streams. Of their sex life little is known but that is enough. In captivity the young ones are droll and frolicsome. They climb the furniture and burrow through solid walls hunting for

Angleworms and Shrimps.[5] In some ways Echidnas
are lower than Platypuses. They look about the same
coming or going.

[1] Or Mullingong or Duck Mole.
[2] I need hardly state that Man is the highest mammal, excepting possibly the Giraffe.
[3] There were plenty of oviparous mammals in the Mesozoic
and nothing was thought of it. But this isn't the Mesozoic.
[4] In his "Zoölogical Notes" (1883), Mr. Arthur Nicols,
F.G.S., F.R.G.S., author of "The puzzle of Life and How It
Has Been Put Together," wrote a long and fascinating account, from first hand observation on the spot, showing that
the Platypus does not lay eggs and would not dream of doing
so. He had actually witnessed the Platypus not laying eggs.
The following year Professor Mosely, President of the Bio-
logical Section, was able to communicate to the meeting of
the British Association, sitting at Montreal, the now historic
message: "Caldwell finds monotremes oviparous, ovum mero-
blastic."
[5] Pet Duck-Billed Platypuses should be kept in old ice-
boxes filled with Australian scenery and rubber squeeges.
There was one at the New York Zoölogical Park in 1922. She
cost $1,400. She was nervous and squirmy.

THE SLOTH

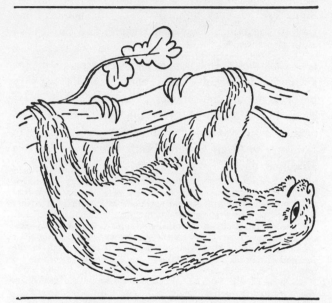

THE Sloth or Jungle Sluggard belongs to the order of Edentates or toothless mammals. He has eighteen teeth. He lives his life upside down, hanging from the branches of cecropia trees in South and Central America.[1] He is perfectly comfortable that way. If the blood rushes to his head nothing happens because there is nothing to work on. Sloths are not active because millions of years ago their ancestors discovered that activity did them no good.[2] Sloths eat cecropia leaves and worry about their troubles.[3] Their forelegs are too long and they have no soles to their feet and the zygoma is nothing to brag of.⁴ They are always wondering whether they feel better or worse.⁵ Sloths are not very impulsive. They do not care one way or the other. They make gentle and inoffensive pets. Baby Sloths hook themselves to one's clothing and stay there. Unhooking baby Sloths is fun for awhile but the novelty soon wears off. Sloths are very particular about the number of their toes. The Ai or Three-toed Sloth is smaller than the Unau or Two-toed Sloth. The Bashful Sloth of Cayenne is becoming extinct. The Giant Ground Sloth of Buenos Aires is already extinct. He was a little too much.

---

¹ The frivolous Sidney Smith went so far as to remark that the Sloth exists in a continual state of suspense, like a curate distantly related to a bishop. Maybe so.

² The notion that the Sloth is almost if not entirely stationary appears to be widespread. From various arm-chair authorities I learn that with Sloths "a few paces is often the journey of a week," that it takes them "many days to climb a tree," and even that they require "whole months" for the same feat. None of this is true, of course. To know the real facts you have to live in the jungle.

³ Sloths are often said to indulge too freely in self-pity. I have never been able to understand what is so awful about self-pity. I may take it up some time, myself.

⁴ One expert asserts, "Their thighs seem almost disjointed from their haunches." And why wouldn't they?

⁵ M. de Buffon was profoundly shocked at the singular conformation of these animals. "One more defect," said he, "and they could not have existed." He regarded them as the most forlorn and wretched of the brute creation, the victims of perpetual pain, suffering perhaps under the special displeasure of Omnipotence. I can't believe that things are as bad as all that. Sloths seem quite cheerful at times.

THE HYENA

HYENAS are pretty hard to bear. They are mentioned by Shakespeare but that doesn't help much. Hyenas prey upon the weak and defenseless. They eat baby Gazelles and Hottentots and old women out gathering firewood.[1] Other animals will not eat the Hyena. They have to draw the line somewhere. Hyenas are inclined to anger, covetousness and gluttony.[2] They are not proud because they have nothing to be proud of. They have bleary eyes and only sixteen toes and no alisphenoid canals. Hyenas slink. Sex does not interest Hyenas a great deal. They would rather be robbing graves. They always do exactly the wrong thing because they make it a lifework.[3] Hyenas laugh but being a Hyena cannot be laughed off. They have their own jokes which do not seem a bit funny to non-Hyenas. The striped Hyena[4] inhabits India,

(149)

Persia,[5] Arabia, Mesopotamia, Abyssinia and Mount Parnassus.[6] The Spotted Hyena is spotted. The Fossil Hyena is found in Great Britain. It takes only three years to become a complete Hyena.[7]

[1] "Hit him again, he's got no friends," is the Hyena's favorite slogan.

[2] It is often said that Hyenas are fiendishly mean for no reason. This is not strictly true. Everything the Hyena does will be found to have some reason, however inadequate.

[3] According to the ancients, Hyenas are male one year and female the next. They aren't.

[4] With his accustomed gallantry, Aristotle remarks, "It is exceedingly rare to meet a female Hyena."

[5] Note that the Persians have both the Hyena and the Nightingale.

[6] The Niam-niams dress in Hyena skins when they dress at all.

[7] The question has been raised whether Hyenas do not suffer at times about being Hyenas. No, they do not. When faced with the self-evident truth that he is a Hyena, it is second nature to a Hyena to deny the whole thing, or rationalize it into a virtue, or quote Nietzsche, or tell you to mind your own business. An occasional Hyena thinks that other Hyenas are rather horrible.

THE BAT

THE Bat is rather a mess. He is a mammal [1] but he flies [2] by means of membranes or parts of umbrellas stretched over his elongated digits and other things.[3] The Bat is pathetic [4] because he has a rudimentary ulna and a tapering tragus and pectoral mammæ. Many Bats have prominent nose-leaves or frills about the muzzle which do not improve their appearance. They keep trying to touch these with their ears and often succeed. Bats can rotate their legs but where's the fun in that? The brain is primitive like that of the Shrew. Bats are frugivorous or insectivorous or sanguivorous or piscivorous. Bats come out at night. During the day they sleep while suspended head downwards in belfries, caves and ruined castles and under the eaves of Queen's College, Cambridge. They can have twins. The skull of the Flittermouse or Common English Bat is concave. The Red or New York Bat enters bedrooms at night and is very erratic. The Flying Fox of the Malay Archipelago sleeps in india-rubber trees and is often mistaken for fruit of unusual size by persons who make that kind of mistake.[5] In order to love Bats one has to be terribly fond of Nature.[6]

[1] The persistent folk-belief that the Bat is not a mammal appears to be based on the theory that the Mule is not a bird—a shrewd bit of reasoning that has temporarily floored more than one savant.

[2] It is really kinder to Bats to call them mammals. If you think of them as birds, their many imperfections are at once apparent; as volant or flying Bulldogs, however, they do very well, indeed.

[3] Aristotle remarks: "Bats, again, if regarded as winged animals, have feet; and, if regarded as quadrupeds, are without them." I cannot support the Stagirite in this passage. When I regard them as quadrupeds, as I have made a point of doing, they still have feet.

[4] None the less, our popular humorists have managed to produce not a few jests at their expense, such as the statement that a Bat in the belfry is worth two in the hair, the serio-comic charge that he (or she) is "an old Bat" and the like.

[5] Among the Wotjobaluks of Southeastern Australia the Bat is called *Ngunungunut*. Having to speak at a banquet, a friend of the author's, who was not quite himself at the time, got up and announced that among the Ngunungunuts the Bat was known as the *Wotjobaluk*. Much to his chagrin, the revelers literally threw him out of the party.

[6] A correspondent wishes to know which is the ugliest Bat. I am unable to choose among the Great Hare-lipped Bat of Paraguay, the Whiskered Bat of Central Europe, the Tube-nosed Bat of Thibet, the Mastiff Bat of the Amazon, the Naked Bat of Malaya and the Chinese Bat, or *Peen-foo*, or *Foo-yeh*, or *Fei-Shoo*. Goodness knows, the ordinary American Pallid Bat, or Hollow-eyed Bat, is trying enough.

THE AARD-VARK

THE Aard-vark or African Earth-pig is neither
here nor there. He has eyes like a Cat and ears
like a Mule and teeth like a Trout and a long viscid
tongue like nothing you ever saw. He also resembles
the Bajjerkeit or Short-tailed Manis of Ceylon and the
Macgillivray Warbler of Central Park. Yet he man-
ages somehow to be very ugly [1] and tiresome. Aard-
varks subsist upon Ants and Termites and are full of
formic acid. Ants are fattening. Aard-varks want their
backs scratched and can find people to do it. Aard-
varks make strange bedfellows. They can burrow into
the hard ground faster than a Boer. [2] Of their mental
operations it would be kinder to say nothing. [3] They
have lucid intervals and certain beliefs which cannot
be gone into here. [4] Aard-varks are nocturnal and shy. [5]

They are afraid of being laughed at or sneered at.[6]
Aard-varks have eighteen toes and twenty-five caudal
vertebræ and the zygoma is all right for a change.
We could do without Aard-varks but things would not
be the same.[7]

[1] There is always the question whether the Aard-vark can
help his looks. I am inclined to think that he could.

[2] In this respect they are not unlike the American Soft-
shelled Clam (Mya arenaria).

[3] The N'jemps of Legumukum have a popular saying, "Don't
be an Aard-vark."

[4] The fact is, I do not know what these beliefs are. And I
may state that it is the last thing I desire to know.

[5] Not all nocturnal animals are shy, by any means. Far
from it.

[6] This is because they cannot sneer back. Young Aard-varks
should be forced to sneer for several hours each day until they
develop a little poise.

[7] I must warn my readers against certain dangers connected
with this book. About an hour from now you will meet a dark
man and begin telling him several hundred things about the
zygoma of the Aard-vark. Two hours later it will turn out that
he is the world's foremost authority on Aard-varks' zygomas
and that his name is Frank Sullivan.